PRAISE FOR

WOMAN OF PRINCIPLE

"Mary Katherine, affectionately known as MK is one of the emerging voices in the world. I've watched her grow within the last 15 years in her wit and wisdom. Her transformational journey is riveting and I am deeply honored to witness her ascent into a brilliant thought leader. Please do yourself a favor and invest buying a box of her books and share them with every woman in your life. They will be tremendously blessed by MK's vulnerability and real breakthrough strategies. Joyce Meyers and Beth Moore, watch out, here comes MK."

SIMON T. BAILEY,

Breakthrough Strategist, Spark Nation Live and author of *Be the Spark*

"Mary Katherine (MK) has written and told a narrative of her life that is inspiring and transformative. The five practices of this book, from her direct experience, offers us all a path of profound awakening to compassion for others and self-love and forgiveness for ourselves. This book is a must-read for both women and men seeking to live a divine life here on earth."

BETTIE SPRUILL,

founder of Ideal Coaching Global

"Brilliant, charismatic and classy. MK approaches everything in life with grace and ease; she always gives it 100% both in her professional and personal life. It is an absolute honor to know her and be part of helping her spread her message."

PATRICIA WERHAHN,

CEO, RedSteel Properties

"Mary Katherine (MK) is masterful at developing high-touch relationships and she is strategic in complex surroundings. She is an accomplished professional and a tremendous leader, community builder and team player. One thing that truly stands out about MK is she operates in her truth and she is authentic, trustworthy and always places the mission of the organization she represents as a top priority. Her loving disposition warms any crowd, and she is a person everyone wants on their team, because she is a winner in every sense of the word."

KIMBERLY GRAMM,

Associate Vice President Innovation
& Entrepreneurship at Texas Tech University

"When my mother introduced me to my greatest mentor 10 years ago, I never imagined that I'd be making over 6-figures as a health coach and be the organizer for a local community group with over 900 members. The patience, wisdom, and guidance that Mary Katherine has given me over the years has transformed more lives than she will ever know. If you are ready to turn your dreams into a reality, Mary Katherine will get you there!"

MICHELLE JOY KRAMER,

Board Certified Health Coach

"One of the many things I love about MK is her heart. She truly loves. She loves people, she loves her work, she loves women, she loves leading by example. She can speak to what it is to be a Woman of Principle because she IS one. And she has made these practices and ways of being a part of the way she engages with the world and everyone in it. I cannot imagine a better guide through these very necessary and practical practices in Becoming a Woman of Principle. It doesn't matter where you are when you find this work, it can support you in practical ways to apply and live from these principles."

JULIE COTTON,

CEO Next Level Improv / International Speaker/Trainer/Author

"God has gifted MK with an amazing heart for women. She loves and leads the women in her Sisterhood Group so well. Always going the extra mile, always encouraging them to live out the God call on their life. I cannot wait to see the lives that will be transformed as she continues to share her God story of freedom through Becoming a Woman of Principle."

DEBBIE LUFFMAN,
Sisterhood Coordinator, Christ Fellowship Church

"For three years, Mary Katherine (MK) served as the Transformational Trainer for The Lodge at Delray Beach, which is a women's sober living community. MK's core message, "What we say to ourselves, quietly or out loud, once or a thousand times, has the power to change the course of our lives." Her commitment was to inspire women to reinvent their lives through the Practices of God first, honesty and implementing prayer and meditation into their everyday living. She is a master at getting women to take a look at how they show up in the world and make a new commitment to live one day at a time – into their divine calling. Through her work, she changed the course of hundreds of women who came through our program during the three years."

SUE MAKENIAN,
Executive Director, The Lodge at Delray Beach

"Mary Katherine Morales is a bold, charismatic, and powerful woman. She was my spiritual mentor and confidant for two years, during which she guided me through my career transformation. She was the catalyst of change in my life. It's thanks to her that I left my career in therapy to become a life coach and transformational trainer. She continues to champion me and all people seeking support in creating their purposeful life."

MILLICENT HUSER,
Transformational Trainer

"Mary Katherine cares deeply about being a positive impact on the lives of others. She is an amazing example of what can be accomplished by staying committed to your goals and living powerfully into your principles. I know there are so many people who will benefit from what MK has to share with the world."

CONNOR LYNCH,
CEO Plastridge Insurance

"Mary Katherine's book is appropriately titled as she is a Woman of Principle. Fueled by her faith and desire to serve others, she shares a story and a commitment that is a true testament of her character."

MICHAEL DESANTI,
Author, New Man Emerging

"The impact Mary Katherine had on my life over the last five years is immeasurable. She is an accomplished professional with an impeccable reputation. Her love for others stems from overcoming the odds and MK is 100% committed; she stands for love, so others experience their own brilliance and live live according to the call upon their lives. Her faith in God is unshakable. MK has the kind of supernatural wisdom required to help others have a breakthrough. The joy and insight she brings to those she serves is remarkable. I am so excited to see what God creates through her in the world."

JOSHUA WILLIAMS,
CEO Legacy Equity Group

"For two years, Mary Katherine taught me skills which I have implemented as a clinical therapist. The most important thing I learned is that language has tremendous power to create or destroy; words become reality. Her wisdom and the practices changed my life."

MEGAN WINCHESTER,
Licensed Clinical Social Worker

"MK has faithfully led others in biblical community through small groups at our church. Her passion and wisdom have encouraged many to grow and mature as followers of Jesus Christ. God has given her a powerful story of grace and strength that has had a tremendous impact on so many lives. It will challenge you to walk in all the freedom that God has waiting for you. I encourage you to read this book!"

RICK MILLER,

Groups Pastor, Christ Fellowship Church

"Mary Katherine is a change agent who not only talks about creating change, she has dedicated herself to it. I have had the honor and privilege of having a front row seat in her life for close to 20 years. She has overcome multiple challenges, faithfully walked through darkness into the light and has truly become a Woman of Principle. She is an encourager whose leadership skills brings people and organizations together for a positive outcome."

TRICIA YOUNGS,

CEO & Clinical Director, The Path to Healing

Becoming
WOMAN
— OF —
PRINCIPLE

Transforming Your Mind.

Living Courageously.

Rising To Your Call.

MARY KATHERINE MORALES

Karen,

Believe in

your Dreams!

MK

Becoming Woman of Principle
Transforming Your Mind, Living Courageously & Rising to Your Call

Editor: Ellena Balkcom, Written on Purpose
Contributing Editor: Lauren Lawley Head, Lawley Head Media
Cover Design and Interior Layout: Kendra Cagle, 5LakesDesign

Library of Congress Control Number: 2020907231

ISBN: 978-1-7347699-0-6 (paperback)
              978-1-7347699-8-2 (kindle)

Mary Katherine Morales
www.WomanofPrinciple.com

Disclaimer:
The information in this book is for personal enlightenment. It is not meant to treat, diagnose or be a substitute for professional medical advice. Though it is presented in good faith, neither the author nor the publisher can assume responsibility or liability for any results, direct or consequential, from the experiment or practical application of this information.

Dedication

To the addict or alcoholic who still suffers in darkness: This story of overcoming unworthiness, shame and the power of addiction is dedicated to you. You are a child of God, worthy of love and peace. I encourage you to walk towards the light of God and experience the truth, freedom and restoration His love promises. The Spirit of Love is always available. It is time to transform your mind, RISE and live the courageous life you've always dreamed.

Future Woman of Principle: You are loved, valuable, eternal and worthy. No matter where you begin this journey — there is a call upon your life. You are divinely significant. It is time for you to RISE and live courageously — every day.

TABLE OF

THE JOURNEY THROUGH HELL TO HOME

Where the Journey Through Hell Begins

A Shift to a New Beginning, So it Seemed

The Darkness Grows

Hitting Rock Bottom

RISING TO YOUR CALL

Living Everyday as a Woman of Principle

Acknowledgments

To God:

"I AM" because you are the alpha and the omega. Words cannot express my thankfulness for your mercy and grace over my life. I will live the rest of my life in gratitude of your unconditional love, and I will declare your goodness — all the days of my life.

To my mom and dad:

Your unconditional love, faithfulness and friendship are the true gifts in my life. You are the light in my life. Always.

To Al, my devoted and loving husband:

Thank you for your unconditional love and faith in me. You are a man of God, my life partner and best friend.

To my love, Mia:

Your love and generous heart create an overwhelming joy in my soul. I thank God for you every day. You are one of 'the' most precious gifts I have ever received.

To my brother:

You've always been my biggest fan, confidant and angel. I hope you know that I have always known 'you' have a sacred call upon your life. You are a man of God, so keep RISING.

To my much-loved and faithful family, best friends, soulmates and mentors:

Thank you for inspiring me to trust God while sharing the most vulnerable and transforming moments of my life. Your prayers lift me beyond my own ability, and I will live the rest of days inspiring others to embrace the journey towards divine significance.

To Skylar, Chloe and Mady, my three beautiful fairy goddaughters:

May you know you are loved, cherished beyond words and worthy of love — always.

To my mentor, Simon T. Bailey:

Your prophetic words over my life have come true. I am deeply grateful for your faithful prayers, honest feedback and words of encouragement over the last 16 years. The dream is now a reality. Exhale.

To Ellena Balkcom, Lauren Lawley Head and Kendra Cagle, three of the most brilliant and creative women I have ever known:

Your supernatural connection with God and your faithfulness helping me achieve my dream means more than words can express.

Preface

In order to get clarity during the blackouts and gaping holes of my life, I've included commentary and input from my family and a few close friends. They will frequently weigh in and share their perspectives, heartbreaking stories, moments of hope and overarching commitment to me becoming who I am today. I want you to understand the consequences of the choices we all make on those who love us, as we face life's most challenging circumstances.

Addiction, dishonesty and a story based on unworthiness impacts the lives of so many people, not just the addict, so it's only fair to have them share their stories. I didn't take this journey through hell to home alone, and I would not have survived and become a powerful, authentic, trusting Woman of Principle without them.

Dear Women of Principle, may you see yourself in every page, as you too, transform your mind, live courageously and rise to the call upon your life.

FROM MARY KATHERINE (M.K.)

"But, we all, with unveiled face, beholding as in a mirror the glory of the Lord, are being transformed into the same image from glory to glory, just as by the Spirit of the Lord."

(2 CORINTHIANS 3:18)

Dear Women of Principle

Welcome to the courageous journey of becoming all God has called you to be. It's the journey of transforming, living and rising as a Woman of Principle — every day. I am so grateful we are taking this powerful journey together.

I believe the time has come for each woman to discover her God-infused purpose, master basic practices and accept the responsibility that her life is a powerful sermon. Everyone you meet is noticing who you are and how you live. Your decisions, big and small, impact everyone you encounter. Beautiful lady, you are lovely, powerful and eternal. It is time to own your divine significance once and for all.

Whether you realize it or not, people are receiving your supernatural messages with every word, every action and every thought. You are either "love energy" or "friction energy" in motion. As we practice putting God First, our minds will transform and our lives will begin to reflect the heart of God. We become beautifully transparent, and the light of God radiates through us.

I wrote the book to encourage all women to embrace the journey from failure to success to divine significance. This cycle repeatedly happens during our lifetime. Most of us stumble, in some way, every day. I like to say that we are perfectly imperfect, and while we embrace being human, we seek supernatural wisdom through a relationship with the Holy Spirit, also known as the Spirit of Love. The distinction for a Woman of Principle is how quickly she recovers from moments of failure and recognizes that through it all, she is always divinely significant. She has nothing to prove.

You, beautiful lady, have a call upon your life, so let's get started.

Woman of Principle, know you:

- *Are a Child of God.*
- *Have the courage to live your dreams — every day.*
- *Have the power to declare your future — every day.*
- *Have the supernatural ability to influence every person you meet — every day.*
- *Can transform into the image of God — every day.*
- *Can master the five practices and super-powerful principles within this book and RISE to the call upon your life.*

I recognize they are bold statements. But they are all 100 percent true based on Holy Scriptures and the promises of God. Depending upon your belief system and life experiences, you may not believe in God's promises entirely. That's okay. This book and the road map ahead of us is a gradual process. Becoming a Woman of Principle is a transcendent process, and whether you define yourself as an inspiring woman rebuilding her life, a successful business executive or a generous stay at home wife and mother, all are welcome.

In my heart, I sincerely believe this is a pivotal moment in time. The world is desperate for women who will stand side by side and hearts wide open, all for love. Through mastering the practices and principles in this book, you will have the influence to create peace where there is discord, reflect hope where there is hopelessness and bring light where there is darkness. We get to decide — here and now — what we want the present moment and the future to look like and begin to practice living as a Woman of Principle every day.

Because I am an honest woman, I will tell you that I wasn't always a fun-loving, authentic, honest and spiritual leader.

On my transformative journey, I was a young woman who had it all: success, beauty, faith in God, popularity and love. That slowly changed over time. I began to trade the life of my dreams for the late-night scene in south Florida's most elite clubs. At a young age, I turned away from the divine call upon my life for local fame and popularity. So-called fame began to turn on me, and the secret during the journey through hell to home, which almost killed me, was that I was suffering from substance use disorder, barely able to get through 24 hours without getting high.

In the pages to come, you will read how the story of unworthiness coupled with dishonesty and a desire to live in pop culture with fast cars, celebrities and drugs almost took my mind and my life. One day at a time, I traded peace, success and significance for a superficial life.

For me to Become a Woman of Principle, I had to master sobriety and overcome the lies of unworthiness and the impact of shame.

Years of self-limiting beliefs, addiction and 100 forms of fear suppressed my healthy mind. The years using drugs and my exposure to extreme situations profoundly changed my core belief system and how I interacted with people. My substance use disorder created a temporary mental illness, and I battled for my physical and spiritual life. I became defensive and consumed with anxiety. In the pages to come, you will find the extreme twists and turns of a young woman desperate to find peace, while waging war against spiritual forces aimed to take her life. However, you will also witness a heartwarming love affair between me, my family and the Holy Spirit. God reached down and saved my life; He restored my soul and my heart.

However, my story is your story. Most of us will have to overcome a significant challenge in our lifetime. The journey to discover my divine significance is only one example of how women of all ages can get lost as we search for our true purpose. The beauty of it all is that with God, we can not only find our way home but create a life beyond our wildest dreams. So, whatever you face in your life, I promise the compelling story of the journey through hell to home, the practices and the supernatural principles to follow will serve as an inspiration for you.

The path to sobriety is rarely a straight line, and mine certainly wasn't. The stories that follow offer a raw look at my failures, relapses and my unwavering desire to get well. I've attempted to share the most pivotal moments, but I acknowledge that there are many significant experiences that did not make the final manuscript, either in the interest of brevity or out of respect for those involved. The people and scenarios I share are accurate to the best of my recollection, although I have occasionally changed someone's name or identifiable characteristics to protect the privacy of others. Honesty is now one of my bedrock practices, and I hope that I have navigated these challenges in a way that reflects that commitment.

In order to get clarity during the blackouts and gaping holes of my life, I've included commentary and input from my family and a few close friends. They will frequently weigh in and share their perspectives, heartbreaking stories, moments of hope and overarching commitment to me becoming who I am today.

Addiction, dishonesty and a story based on unworthiness impacts the lives of so many people, not just the addict, so it's only fair to have them share their stories. I didn't take this journey through hell to home alone, and I would not have survived and become a powerful, authentic, trusting Woman of Principle without them.

Through the grace of God, my Journey through Hell to Home ended almost two decades ago. Although it was the most challenging time in my life, I am grateful for every moment. Today, I live with my heart wide open, and **I am a Stand for Love – everywhere, every day, with everyone.**

On most days, I experience great joy and treat everyone – rich or poor, CEO or stay-at-home mom – exactly the same. I choose respect and compassion because I know that every human being will have to face the kind of challenge that causes them to question God's love, their divine purpose and perhaps, their very life. My commitment is to live my life in a way that helps every person have the opportunity to face their challenges with dignity, overcome the odds, rise to their calling, and then pay it forward.

People often ask me how I *became* M.K. 2.0.

My transformation and what is now the solid rock of my foundation stem from five life-changing practices, which led to living supernatural principles. One primary practice, however, is the bedrock of everything I say and do. This practice of becoming beautifully transparent embodies who I am as a Woman of Principle, which has opened the door to every opportunity and has allowed me to create a life beyond my wildest dreams by rarely compromising on this core commitment: *I am an honest woman.* I am not faultless, but I am intentionally honest. It's my stand for love — every day, with everyone.

My sobriety, my connection to the Holy Spirit, my relationships and my divine significance depend upon my commitment to be honest. And heartfelt, brutal and transparent honesty about the hard-won journey through unworthiness, fear and addiction is the baseline in the chapters of *Becoming Woman of Principle: Transforming Your Mind, Living Courageously and Rising to Your Call.*

As a society, I deeply believe the greatest addiction facing the human race today is the disease of dishonesty. It has created massive chaos far and wide. It is creating confusion in the workplace and dividing families and communities. It is the tool the spirit of evil uses to kill, steal and destroy. As Women of Principle, it is time for us to stand for love and take back what was rightfully given to us by God. When we choose to lie, even a white lie, the strength, power and context of our mind, our brain and our soul begin to diminish. With every drop of black tea that is dropped into a pitcher of clear water, the purity changes. Over time, the water is no longer transparent. It becomes gray, then light black, and eventually, it *becomes* tea.

Our minds, with every thought and every word we speak, change the circumstances of our lives and the context of our soul. Becoming victorious through the practice of running with champions is another practice that will challenge you to hand-pick your "core five" tribe, develop your voice, and step into a championship role. Each practice has spirit-filled principles. They all have the power to radically transform the woman who has the courage to implement them into her daily life. You get to choose which practice reflects your stand for love. Why? Because what we practice, we become. You will become masters of each practice, then turn towards others and teach them.

Thank you for walking with me through each chapter, as God unveils the divine revelation of five practices that will guide you toward principles by which I hope you will choose to live. We all have our own addictions, vices or strongholds that derail our dreams, wreck our relationships and steal our peace. However, there is hope in God and help in the application of these principles. Dear Women of Principle, may you see yourself in every page, as you too, transform your mind, live courageously and rise to the call upon your life. At the end of this book, your transforming mind will be ready and equipped to live courageously. It's time to rise and walk according to God's purpose for your life!

By His grace and for His glory,

M.K.

Prologue

Like a stolen moment of people-watching where you find yourself captivated by the actions, mannerisms and general state of other people, I sat outside of myself staring in disbelief at the state of my life, my physicality and the hotel room I found myself holed up in. The once richly decorated, upscale room was in disarray: the bed unmade, the tasteful pictures removed from their hooks and turned backward, so the cameras that I was sure were hidden inside couldn't see me.

I couldn't remember how I'd gotten here. I was barely functioning after days of scarcely eating and sleeping. I didn't know how my skeletal, 100-pound body found the energy to cause such damage.

Though the past days had come and gone, with one fading into another, I knew that the damage I caused this time was more than physical. It was more than spiritual. It was a battle to the death, with God and me on one side and the Devil and his minions on the other. But in my life journey, the Devil went by a different name, and his name was "the Great Destroyer."

The morning light intruded through the curtains, taunting me with the possibility that today might be the day that I could muster enough courage to go home, where my loving husband and daughter waited for me.

To look at me on this day, you would have sadly dismissed me as just another low-class, uneducated addict. But I wasn't. I had it all — youth, beauty, education, financial success, and, most importantly, love. But that was before my soul began to deteriorate, one day at a time. My face was drawn, with hollow cheeks and sunken eye sockets. My chin had small red sores from stress and lack of nutrition. I desperately tried to hide the scars on my face by wearing heavy foundation, full make-up, and lip gloss. My bloodshot eyes were swollen from crying. The dark circles under my eyes told the story of a scared, lost woman rushing headlong toward death, insanity and destruction. My once beautifully blonde, curly hair was now disheveled and tightly pulled away from my face, and my pathetic, tiny body was covered in clothes scented with perfume and booze. I disgusted myself.

I had been hiding out for days trying to decide when I would start communicating with my exasperated husband, Al. I was wracked with guilt. Such a gentle soul didn't deserve to marry someone with such heartbreaking issues.

I picked up the receiver to call him, but it seemed unusually weighty. Were phones always so heavy? I knew I had stayed in this place far too long. With barely any sleep, I felt death's presence oppressing me. At $150 a night, this was no roach motel — and too many days of denying the maids admission to clean made me feel as if I was under suspicion. Management must know something was going on. It was only a matter of time before they would pound on the door for answers.

Attempting to practice rigorous honesty, I finally called Al and told him, for the first time in several days, I was ready to come home. He agreed to rescue me, but he didn't sound relieved. Anxiously, I packed my suitcase. I wanted to clean the room, ashamed of the mess I was leaving for the hotel staff. Where would they begin?

With indescribable suspicion and shame, I craned my neck out the door, making sure the halls were clear. I needed to bolt from the room so the housekeepers wouldn't see me.

Instead of taking the elevator, I sprinted toward the staircase where there would be less human activity. Bounding down several flights, the luggage hit both walls with reckless abandon, dragging behind this frail, sick-looking young woman. At the bottom of the stairwell, I parked my suitcase and perched upon it, waiting for Al to arrive.

I thought the back door would be safer. Instead, it turned out to be the staff entrance, and the morning shift was arriving. Shiny, well-adjusted people streamed through in their starched uniforms with rehearsed smiles on their faces. Technically, I was still a guest of the hotel, so I suppose they had to pretend not to notice that I was a hot mess. Although my broken demeanor cried out for compassion, I knew they looked at me and wondered what on earth was wrong.

Thirty long minutes passed, and Al still hadn't come to rescue me, so I called again. He reassured me he was on the way.

I took a deep breath to relieve some of my overwhelming anxiety, thinking to myself, *"In a few minutes, I will be out of danger. I won't have to look over my shoulder anymore or wonder if I will sleep tonight. When the buzz wears off, I can take a shower, put on my favorite pajamas and slip into my bed. I will try to eat before I fall into a deep sleep.*

My body will once again begin to heal itself from many long days of abuse.

Al's black truck pulled into the lot, and I was ashamed for my new husband to see me; the once-beautiful, polished bride he fell in love with now a broken and disheveled woman. Through the windshield, I watched his face change from disbelief to sadness. His heart must have torn wide open as he saw me leaning against my suitcase for support. I stumbled over to the truck and tried to lift the bag.

Al got out and threw it in the backseat. "I have conditions," he said matter of factly, buckling me in like a helpless baby. Our eyes connected, which felt embarrassing and beautiful at the same time. "You can either go to treatment, or you can go back upstairs to hell." He had packed clean clothes for me, which explained the other piece of luggage in the backseat.

I was furious as we pulled onto the highway ramp. I was *not* going to treatment! I tried to explain that all I needed was to go home and sleep it off. I knew I could get sober on my own. I promised him it would never happen again.

His cell phone rang. Al answered it and told the person on the other end that I was not willing to get help.

"Who are you talking to?" I barked.

"Susan is a woman who is willing to help you get addiction treatment," he said, pointedly. "She wants to speak to you." I was appalled Al thought I needed medical attention but took the phone, nevertheless. This Susan woman tried to coax me into treatment, saying I needed to surrender. She didn't know who I was. She didn't know I was smart and educated enough to see through her manipulative "sales pitch." I had kicked this drug thing before – on my own terms – and I would do it again now.

Journney
THROUGH
HELL
TO HOME

Chapter One

I found out the hard way that not having solid spiritual principles hinders everything else in your life. I had every advantage a person can be given: a loving family, wealth, education, and beauty. No one could understand why a girl with my background would willingly throw away her late twenties and early thirties – the prime years of her life.

When I was little, my dad worked for Allstate Insurance and moved us from Chicago to St. Petersburg, Florida. All four of us – my father John, mother Sandy, my little brother Johnny, and I – quickly fell in love with the state of sunshine, palm trees, orange groves and beaches.

Unlike my Illinoisan family, landlocked away from ocean tides, swimming pools and sunshine, I was a water bug and had a natural talent for swimming. There was a drive within to excel at the sport, and I performed my swim laps with dedication and focus as far back as first grade.

My stroke was the butterfly, and my dad spent endless hours at the pool, helping me to improve. If I came in second, I was mad and inconsolable for days at a time. It wasn't in my nature to come in second.

This dedication to being the best was contested by my second-grade teacher, Mrs. Miller, who became fed up with my stubborn unwillingness to follow directions. One day she called my mom and asked, "What is wrong with Mary Katherine? She just will not listen in class. Does the child ever do anything without discussion?"

"No, she does not," was the reply.

Eventually, my teacher figured out the problem and called our house again.

"I think Mary Katherine acts out because she can't hear me."

Her diagnosis sent me off to auditory testing sites. Seated in a cold glass bubble, I remember the ear doctor slipping a big pair of 1970s-era earphones on my little blonde head. BEEP, BEEP, BEEP went the sounds in the headset. I raised my right or left hand, indicating in which ear I heard the noises. I tried my best to answer correctly, but, sadly, this was one contest in which I wouldn't take first place. The audiologist concluded I had a hearing impairment of such severity that I was categorized as legally deaf.

Sometimes I went to medical offices two or three times a week, sometimes every day. At one point, I went every day after school to maintain a balance between my hearing and the buildup of liquids that would fill my ear canal while shutting me off from hearing my family, teachers and friends. I had dozens of surgeries in a short period of time. The doctors put tubes in my ears to open the canals.

Nothing really came of all this time on the operating table, and my hearing never really improved. Being partially deaf left me out of conversations at school. I was a chameleon of sorts, often unable to comprehend what people were saying but trying to guess and adapt. I created the story that kids were always talking about me when they would look my way and laugh.

This was the beginning of the internal narrative of I am not worthy nor good enough.

My discomfort likely drove me to become a competitive swimmer, where I didn't need to hear underwater to fit in with the crowd. I was on an even playing field when in the pool. Having to put Vaseline and lamb's wool in my ears and a tight rubber swim cap over my head made me stand out, but being different pushed me towards achieving greater successes from this point forward in sports, schoolwork, and later, my career choices.

My mom recalled:

It was very difficult for Mary Katherine. I did not realize it at the time. In second grade, she came home from Catholic school and said, 'Mom, what do you think your cross is?' I asked her what she meant. She said, 'Everyone has a cross to bear, and I know what mine is. It's my loss of hearing.' She really struggled with it. As her mother, my heart broke to hear my seven-year-old talk about this heavy burden. She knew then she was different from her friends. She was heartbroken because she felt alone. She loved playing games and being in relationship with people. She just couldn't hear them to really connect.

Despite my winning record and my love of competitive swimming, I began to narrate a story of unworthiness, which led to low self-esteem. As a young girl, I experienced what it was like to feel very alone in a world where words were jumbled and confusing and sound was muffled. I no longer wanted to use lamb's wool and Vaseline in front of my classmates, so I used the excuse of looking like a boy to sway my parents to let me quit swimming. And despite my long, curly blonde hair and flair for stylish, feminine clothes, my back was muscular and strong, defined with a V-shape, which didn't make me feel feminine. My dad thought I was nuts. "How could *you ever* look like a boy, Mary Katherine?" he asked in disbelief.

But I knew I needed to stay involved in sports in order to fit in and remain connected with my friends. Plus, I loved athletics. All of it – the art of competition, the thrill of winning and the sting of defeat. It motivated me, as it does even today. I was also a cheerleader from first grade through college. Being on the squad meant the world to me.

My competitive nature probably kept me alive in my fight against addiction – that and the grace of God. Off and on over a decade, I was prey to the demons that roamed the earth, and I was defenseless against temptation. Others may have the capacity to walk away from the lure of the late-night scene. Because I suffered from the story of unworthiness, lacking spiritual wisdom and discipline, I had a different experience. Despite the discouraging pattern of four failed rehab treatments and multiple relapses that marked those years, I always held onto the hope and sense of connection I found in God when I was a little girl. The fact that an addict can even have a relationship with God might surprise some, but I loved God even in the darkest hours of my active addiction.

This desperate letter, written during the height of my illness, illustrates God's presence in my life during that time.

Dear Mom and Dad,

I can't seem to quit writing. I only wish I could talk to you again, to tell you how sick I really am right now. But the phone in the hotel won't call long distance.

For some (and I pray I'm not one of them) the addiction envelops every cell. It saturates your body with enough craving and chemicals that it is almost impossible to stop. I'd say that in a way, I've become "brainwashed" by what I've seen, heard, felt, and done while high. It transforms me into another person – a woman I do not know or like. The woman

that is sitting here writing this is afraid of living
because, in my opinion, my life is a failure and has
lacked any real success in the last five years.
I just drift from conversation to conversation,
switching the narrative to fit the person in front of
me. There is a voice within me that wants to scream,
"Help me, I am dying!" Yet there's another voice
telling me that I can get sober – I can quit if I just
try one more day. Just for today – I will listen to
the voice that tells me to hold on to God.

Oh, how I miss you, Mom and Dad. I miss going to
church and knowing Jesus is standing next to me. I
am going to lie down now ... more later...

—Mary Katherine

My cry to God and to my family wasn't always so dramatic and painful. I have so many wonderful memories. Overall, my life has been blessed beyond measure. As a little girl, I went to church every Sunday and attended a Catholic school through eighth grade. I learned about Jesus from the nuns, most of whom were very nice. They were soft-spoken, polite, and told stories about how much God loved us. As a little girl, my perception was that God did a lot for us and that He loved kids. However, I also had a feeling that bad things happen to people who sinned or behaved badly. There were times I was afraid of what might happen to me, because I knew I wasn't perfect — and that I was a sinner according to the examples they taught in Sunday school.

My family worshipped in typical Catholic fashion. We attended Mass every week and celebrated holidays like Christmas and Easter. For Christmas, Mom always went overboard to make sure it was a wonderful day. My brother and I would come out from our bedrooms Christmas morning, and the entire floor would be covered in beautifully wrapped gifts. We tore into the toys and spent the day laughing and playing with everything we received. My parents constantly provided joy-filled holidays. Easter was especially filled with happiness, because we always had neighborhood friends in to celebrate this holiday. We would all play games like "Egg Toss" and "Easter Egg Hunt." Tirelessly working behind the scenes of all our family holiday gatherings was my mom. She always made an extraordinary effort to create theme parties that would remain in our memories forever.

During my childhood, I couldn't have asked for a more loving and nurturing family, but I still sought solace in Jesus.

As a little girl, I used to close my eyes and pray that Jesus would come and sit on my bed, so we could talk about healing my hearing impairment. I was tired of feeling different, of not understanding what the teachers and my friends were saying to me, and of having to take baths and not showers so my ears wouldn't get wet. *Jesus can help me with that or anything,* I hoped.

Chapter Two

My dialogue with Jesus continued uninterrupted until I experienced the opposite side of the spiritual spectrum when I turned fourteen.

To celebrate my birthday, I invited seven girlfriends over for a slumber party. A sun-filled day at the beach turned into more splashing in the pool at our house. Mom and Dad made burgers on the grill, we shared birthday cake, and I unwrapped gifts from my friends.

Evening rolled in, and I decided it was time to kick it up a notch. I walked into the room with my arms full of board games. "What do you want to play?" I asked.

"What's a Ouija board?" inquired one girl.

I had no idea. It was still shrink-wrapped, a leftover present from last December. We moved everything out of the way and made a comfortable place next to the bed. The box's instructions told us to light candles and sit in a circle. We were directed to ask questions to the board, and it would either answer by moving the pointer to the words "Yes" or "No," or spell out more complicated answers. Several people were supposed to hold onto the pointer, but it was supposedly navigated by spirits beyond this earthly realm.

For a group of eight teenage girls, it seemed like the perfect game for a slumber party; it was exciting and a little spooky. We knew it was an interactive game but didn't understand the dangers that came with it.

Quite a few of us touched the pointer with our fingertips and started asking the board questions. At the time, I had a secret crush on Tim Taylor, a cute football player with dark hair and blue eyes.

"Does Mary Katherine like Tim Taylor?" my friend asked. The pointer went over to "Yes." Everyone laughed, surprised at its accuracy. One girl accused me of manipulating the board so it would go where I wanted it to go. She asked, "Is Mary Katherine moving the Ouija arrow?" and it went to "No."

"Is someone else moving the board?"

"Yes."

"Who's moving the board?"

This is when the so-called game turned creepy. There was trepidation and nervousness among my circle of friends as we stared at one another in the dimly lit room. The arrow moved to the letter "D." And then slowly to the letter "E." I felt my palms getting sweaty. I tried to tell myself that it was ridiculous. Someone else was doing it.

The arrow moved to the letter "V." At that point, everyone else started getting scared. We had secured the board on some books, and our knees were touching each other. I could feel the other girls beginning to shake. As the arrow shifted to the letter "I," the intensity in the room elevated again.

As the arrow landed on the letter "L," my friends jumped up and sprinted from the room. They were screaming as though a burglar had just smashed through the window, threatening to harm us all. I was the last out and was blocked by our Doberman Pinscher standing in the doorframe. He was barking like a dog consumed with intense fear.

"Sable, it's me! It's me!" I yelled. She seemed to be reacting to the Ouija board and wouldn't let me pass. I was terrified down to my core. The hairs on my arms stood on end, and I was covered in goosebumps. It felt like there was someone or something evil in my room that wasn't there moments earlier. Whether there was truly something evil in my room that night, or it was the insanity of teenage girls screaming and running down the hallway in a flash mob, or something darker and more sinister at work, I'll never know.

My mom remembers the evening well.

I can still see Mary Katherine in the living room that night. The expression on her face was like one of those movies where a person tries to get the Devil out of his body. She was terrified beyond terrified. I didn't realize at the time how bad it was or how it would impact her later. It was just one of those scary things that kids do when they're sitting around and talking about ghost stories. Looking back on it now, it's really like an evil spirit attached itself to her that night. That night forward, for several years to come, Mary Katherine was petrified to fall asleep and kept the lights on.

The Holy Scriptures reveal that pagan worship is the spearhead of all demonic activity. I didn't know this to be true at the time but had always felt like there was something out there — a spiritual force battling against God and against us — and now I was convinced of it.

I was always prone to nightmares, but the Ouija board scare intensified my dream life.

The recurring nightmare of a lady in a dark mansion trying to take my soul and those of my friends lasted for four years, until I went to college. This nightmare only intensified my fear of the dark and falling asleep. Too often, my mom would wake up to see the light on in my bedroom at 2:00 a.m., finding me writing poems and stories, doing anything to keep myself awake and away from that demonic presence haunting my dreams.

But later, with the introduction of alcohol and pills, my nightmares crossed over into my waking hours. I wasn't a drug user in high school, but in my senior year, when I started dating a guy named Chris, we occasionally smoked pot together, which re-introduced a distressing spirit into my life. One night, when my parents were gone, we lit up a joint and smoked it. Within minutes, I felt like a demonic spirit had entered the house. The hair on my arms stood straight on end, and I became chilled to the bone. I was afraid to turn around, certain I would see the demonic spirit walking towards me. This was the first time I experienced this force outside of my dreams, and it terrified me. The aura in the house shifted, and I felt like a wicked energy force was surrounding me on every side. It transpired in slow motion. I could feel the man from my dreams coming toward me in the hallway. Even though I couldn't physically see him, I could sense his presence flowing toward me. Tears filled my eyes as I said to Chris, "He's here."

"You are not welcome here!" I shouted. I walked toward the hallway where I knew the spirit was standing, instead of walking toward Chris. "In the name of Jesus, get out!" I could hear Chris laughing behind at me at first, but he stopped when he realized I was serious. The phantom spirit left the house — and so did Chris. I didn't want to be around him. I needed time to pray and ask God for forgiveness. I had placed myself in grave danger by smoking pot. I knew chemicals were referred to in the Bible as partaking in witchcraft. Petrified, that night I slept with the light on, in my brother's room in his extra twin bed.

It's possible my hallucination was enhanced by the weed. But I still believe there was something in that moment that terrified me, some wicked energy inside the house that night. What I was too young to understand was I had opened a Pandora's Box that would haunt me, influence my behavior and affect my soul for years. These, I believe, were the early steps in what would become my journey through hell and my fight to get back home.

The last nightmare happened during my freshman year of college, when the demonic being turned his focus on my family. It said one night, "If you don't give me your soul, I'm going to take your dad." At that point, my father entered the dream, and he and I fought the evil spirit before the altar of a church. I remember my dad proclaiming in a loud voice, "This is it! You don't get my soul, and my daughter is not giving you hers!" My dad stood, as the spiritual leader in my life, defending me at the altar inside the house of God. For the first time, the demon retreated and seemed to relinquish its demand for power over me.

I called my loving father. Of course, he was just fine. I shared the details of the dream, and we agreed the nightmares were finally over. And after five-and-a-half years, I was set free. It never occurred again.

Although the recurring dreams of the demonic man left me that night, I did not realize my exposure to unclean spirits later in life would come in all shapes, sizes and containers, including pills, powders, liquids and solids. To my surprise, nightclubs, late-night parties and trance music would once again swing open the Pandora's Box I closed as a teenager, taking me a few more steps on the hellacious journey that would become my life.

The Bible says, "Our enemy, the Devil, prowls around like a roaring lion looking for someone to devour" (1 Pet. 5:8). I believe Satan's evil spirits usually infiltrate people through their minds, and Scripture is replete with instructions for appropriately managing our minds by controlling our thoughts through meditating on the Word of God.

By using mind-altering substances, I put myself at risk. I knew they introduced chaos in my soul and produced confusion, fear and, ultimately, contact with unclean spirits – both on earth and in the spiritual realm.

WHERE THE *Journney* THROUGH HELL BEGINS

---

*"The only way shame is healed is if
it is brought into the light."*

—MARY-ALICE ISLEIB

Chapter Three

It was the early Eighties, and drugs were just starting to enter the public discussion. Nancy Reagan was beginning the "Just Say No" campaign. At school, we were forced to watch a film featuring hippies doing acid. My friends and I laughed, watching the illustrations of long-haired, greasy, unwashed relics from the Sixties tripping out on hallucinogens. Bugs climbed all over the camera lens, trying to teach us what dropping acid looked like. A bad narrator warned us of the side effects. The film meant nothing to us, other than an opportunity to stop doing classwork and laugh at hippies.

This wasn't the stuff being discussed in my home. My parents didn't talk about challenging subjects like sex or drugs. I'm not blaming them, but I was totally unprepared for life outside of our home. I lived in a completely sheltered environment where dangerous subject matter was left unspoken.

At the same time, I was mildly experimenting with alcohol, learning how to manage a part-time job, and I had the added responsibility of supervising my younger brother. Johnny was a freshman during my senior year, and he loved the fact that he never had to take the bus to school. I was his ride; I was also his ticket to all the upper-classman parties. Being a good-looking, blonde charmer, Johnny was always popular at school. The night the Homecoming Queen was to be crowned during halftime, Johnny got the whole freshman football team to rally around and vote for me. I was his hero, and in that moment, he was mine.

I cheered for the first part of the game, and at halftime went back with the other girls to change from our uniforms into our homecoming dresses. I wore a baby blue strapless dress with white ruffles that complimented my long, blonde curls.

Those of us nominated were driven back out onto the field to the fantastic roar of the crowd. We sat atop a convertible and waved at the fans in the stands. I felt popular and beautiful, and it was quite a rush. For a moment, my story of unworthiness and being separate from others was silent. I was at peace.

Each girl was announced with tidbits of information about her hobbies and interests. I stood between Julie and Sally, and I held my breath in anticipation. Last year's Homecoming Queen, a redhead named Michelle, held the crown in her hands.

I squinted to see my supportive family in the stands. Mom and Dad were cheering. Johnny and his teammates were in their freshman football uniforms, chanting my name. I smiled with joy.

Michelle opened the envelope and paused. The longest pause, ever. In that moment, my peace was gone, and my mood went from excitement to fear. I thought, *if I win, these girls are going to hate me.* My insecurities were forgotten the next moment when the announcer read my name: "Mary Katherine. Mary Katherine Sabol!"

I won. I was crowned Homecoming Queen. The next hour of my life was an exhilarating time of congratulations and celebratory hugs. I was doted upon by everyone except my selfish boyfriend Chris, who wasn't about to share the spotlight. Standing off to the side in his tight jeans and Black Sabbath T-shirt, Chris looked agitated and impatient with the whole scene.

You might think after a disastrous end to that evening that included Chris being wasted and a total narcissistic jerk that we would have been finished for good, but we dated off-and-on into my freshman year of college. My shame of loving a cruel man took its toll on my heart and mind. Now, looking back at how I got so far off track, I realize that I lacked both a connection to God and true feelings of self-worth and self-love. Even then, I was searching for something outside of me to fill the void deep within my soul. Beautiful readers, can you relate?

Have you ever questioned your self-worth, which led you to make poor choices?

My mom weighs in:

Mary Katherine and Chris finally broke up their freshman year in college, and our sweet daughter returned. She surrendered her peace of mind and her morals dating him. It was terrible to watch Mary Katherine sacrifice her all-American-girl virtues for a head-banger who treated her so poorly. She never dated anyone like him again.

A SHIFT TO A
NEW
Beginning
SO IT SEEMED

"New beginnings are often disguised
as painful endings."

—LAO TSU

Chapter Four

Some people hate college; some love it. For me, college was the time of my life. I experienced self-respect and joy. My college boyfriends were smart, successful and treated me like a lady. For two-and-a-half years I dated Bobby, a super-cute, marvelous, nerdy engineer – but a cool nerd, the total opposite of the handsome and dangerous Chris. Mom and dad liked Bobby, though they knew he was just a college crush.

Bobby and I had so much fun together, dancing at the clubs or sharing great meals poolside with other couples. We spent hours together studying in the library, and many nights cheering for our much-loved sports teams at our favorite hotspots. Bobby and I had a wholesome and healthy relationship, but we were just too young to see how good we had it.

I did well in school, maintaining a "B" average. At first, I was a Liberal Arts major, but later I turned my focus to Communications and Marketing. I joined a sorority, Zeta Tau Alpha, and had many female friends inside that sorority house. I made the college cheerleading squad, and I enjoyed popularity through cheerleading for football and basketball. I was nominated all four years for homecoming court, and I spent a lot of time volunteering for my favorite charitable organizations. It was perfect, just like a movie scene about how college should be — from all-night study sessions downstairs cramming for exams to pillow fights to break the late-night doldrums, interrupted by inspirational chats about who we hoped to become after graduation. Being in the sorority was a never-ending social scene.

When I wasn't with Bobby, my sorority sisters, or the student government, I was cheerleading. We practiced diligently five days a week in preparation for the game on day six. I loved everything about being a college cheerleader, from the pep rallies to the performances.

It was such a perfect time in my life. I had a boyfriend who loved me and whom my parents liked; I was doing well in school, and I had a rich and positive social life that didn't involve pot or alcohol. Even my relationship with God became stronger. I thought God had answered my prayers. I was happy and had a deep sense of love and belonging, no longer feeling like an outsider. I had peace of mind.

One night, Bobby and I visited my best friend, Amy, at the University of Florida. Over the course of the evening, she started going on and on about this pill called Ecstasy. She'd been doing it for years and wanted us to join in on the fun. I was resistant. I had avoided pot since high school and felt no need to start that insanity again. I was totally drug-free with very little alcohol intake for four years.

Yet, she persisted. She told me to try half a pill. There we were, in her boyfriend's fraternity house, going back and forth about this stupid little pill. Ultimately, I caved and popped it in my mouth. No big deal, right?

I leaned back into the couch and waited to feel the effect of the drug. It didn't take long. Staring up at the ceiling fan, I thought, *"That is so cool. It just goes around and around and around."* I had never felt so relaxed and comfortable in my skin. I felt beautiful and confident. I felt what I imagined to be "at peace." Honestly, it was a great night. I had never experienced someone else's skin feeling so comfortable next to mine. Holding Bobby's hand was incredible. My senses became unusually heightened, and my ability to express my thoughts and emotions became so effortless that I wanted to feel that way more often. I sat with Amy for hours, talking about life and openly sharing my secret hopes and dreams in a way I had never expressed before.

After that night, it became my constant companion. It was a fun, social drug and a way for me to go out with people and connect. My friends drank a lot, so I took half a pill and always felt part of the group.

Now in my final two semesters in college, and with cheerleading practices over, the party scene started to fill the void in my schedule. Even though I was already a social person, "E" made me feel more alive. I didn't look into the dangers of MDMA. Most described it as the hottest thing in searching for happiness through chemistry. I just remember my friend John telling me that Ecstasy was legal in his home state of Alabama, claiming he used to pay a $10 cover charge to get into a bar where he got a drink coupon and an MDMA pill.

I thought, *well, if they're giving it away at bars in Alabama, there must not be anything wrong with it.*

Ecstasy became popular with all my girlfriends and college buddies. Looking back, it became a dangerous epidemic. Thousands of seemingly smart, high-performing college students became part of this weekend subculture.

We got dressed up, had dinner, took some Ecstasy, and went dancing inside warehouses where late-night raves were all the rage. Girls were dressed in psychedelic outfits, sucking on pacifiers, wearing their hair in pigtails. It was shocking! At the other extreme, there were beautiful young women dressed like movie stars, smiling and enjoying the club's atmosphere. Guys were hallucinating in the corners of the room while dancing wildly to loud music. It was a spectacle encompassing all walks of life, including me. Though I considered myself normal compared to those I described – I was still involved in this subculture, dancing center stage, on Ecstasy, and loving the entire experience. The music came from gigantic speakers and bounced off the walls. I could feel the bass in my heart space. The extensive laser light shows in hues of red, blue, and magenta created waves of emotions among the crowd; the community would cheer, in awe of what the DJ and light technician could create. Circus acts such as tightrope artists and acrobats in body paint occupied the air space above the crowd to keep the audience engaged. Exotic and strange performers danced, using trancelike gestures inside cages and behind silhouette screens. Intoxicated, everyone appeared to have the freedom to dance, laugh, and be their true selves. We *did* stare at the strangest of the rave-goers, yet they really didn't care what anyone thought of their hair, what they wore, their rhythm or lack thereof, and from that perspective, they were appealing.

As the sun rose, everyone went back to their respective homes. The next day, we got up and carried on with our lives. Most of the time, our meager hangovers and few other repercussions allowed us to live like those who went to bed at a decent hour. Yet I knew, from watching the severest outsiders and the most extreme spectators inside those warehouses, that some didn't fare quite so well. It was a foreshadowing of my own future.

Chapter Five

Though my college life was amazing, as the saying goes, all good things must come to an end. Bobby and I broke up before senior year. I was progressing towards graduation from UCF, but during my last semester, I went out dancing with my girlfriend Lauren one night. We headed to a trendy club called JJ Whispers where there was an attractive police officer named Mitch working security at the door. With his handsome face, big blue eyes, and sexy uniform that fit like a glove, I was hooked.

After a few weeks of flirting with Officer Mitch, I gave him my phone number. Once we started dating, I decided there was no point in trying to hide my partying from him, even if he was a cop.

Because his assignment was stopping gangs and not narcotics, he had a lax attitude towards my recreational use. Though he said he couldn't do it himself, he'd look the other way if I decided to partake occasionally in the party scene.

Mitch and I had a ball together. We went on vacations. We loved the beach. We loved family gatherings. We went dancing with friends, cheered on our football team during tailgate parties, and had season tickets for our favorite professional basketball team, the Orlando Magic. Mitch and I never fought — we were a great couple.

During the final semester of my senior year in college, I came home and told my mom I had a job, but there was a chance she might not be happy with it.

"You're not working at Hooters, are you?" she joked, which was hilarious, because yes, that's precisely where I had found employment. The day I graduated from college in the spring of 1992, I was promoted from waitress/bartender to marketing manager for two stores.

While working at Hooters, I befriended a girl named Allison. She introduced me to her closest friends. They were nine gorgeous girls who often competed in the Hawaiian Tropic pageants and fitness challenges. The best thing was they were as nice as they were charming and beautiful on the outside.

We worked together at Hooters. We were attractive young women who were truly living the dream: residing in the chicest areas, making lots of money, driving expensive cars, buying designer clothes, and getting into the most exclusive clubs. We worked and played hard. As the best of friends, we had many good memories together hosting wonderful dinner parties, playing volleyball, traveling to beautiful places where the sunset takes your breath away, to snuggling on the couch watching our favorite movies. But our collective group took a sharp left turn when we started putting other substances in the mix. Collectively, we went from good to bad. Our routine each weekend quickly changed. We did pills to get ourselves charged up on the dance floor, and once we danced the night away, we would head back to someone's house and continue the party.

However, my cop boyfriend was getting in the way of my partying. When he proposed to me, I told him I needed some time to think it over. He didn't like raves or large nightclubs. He didn't love trance or house music, and some of my so-called friends didn't want to have a cop as part of our scene. Mitch didn't want to have dinner or social conversations with any of my circle. Who would blame him, right? After some time, and emotional confusion, I said "yes" to his proposal. That just thrilled my parents; they loved Mitch and were delighted I had found someone so kind, responsible and hard-working.

Unfortunately, I eventually started to feel differently about his job. It was becoming more dangerous, so I broke off the engagement. I was young and terrified I would lose him to gang violence. My family thought I was ridiculous. "Are you nuts?" they asked me, with good reason. "This guy is a great family man, incredibly loyal, a hard worker…"

I knew all of this and loved Mitch, but I wasn't ready to get married. He was five years my senior and ready for the next step. I had different ideas about what the future would hold, yet I had no clue what was actually in store as my life took a hard turn, hell-bound into an abyss of destruction.

I went from social using to a temporary drug-induced mental illness. I was searching for that perfect pharmaceutical combination. It doesn't exist.

The consequences of the weekend partying started to catch up with me. While my girlfriends laughed and joked around while under the influence of alcohol, I became silent, introverted and reclusive. Maybe my chemical makeup was different, because when I started mixing medications, my body and my mind said, "I can't handle this." I began feeling left out again, just like when I was a child with a hearing impairment. Once more, I felt like the outsider and believed my best friends didn't want me around anymore. The story of unworthiness returned. Soon, paranoia and fear became my frequent and unwelcome companions.

During this time, there was no such thing as research for "substance use disorder" or public campaigns that supported people suffering from addiction. To be a beautiful woman with the disease of addiction was a curse, and society was absolutely brutal to anyone who admitted they had an alcohol or substance use disorder. I knew to remain silent in my illness.

One night, I tiptoed over the sleeping bodies crashed out on the couches, floors, or any flat surface in the house. I grabbed the wall for balance and managed to stumble into a bathroom. I stared at my sad reflection in the mirror over the sink. My beautiful, long, curly hair was pulled back in a tight bun, which was a sign of my life descending into misery. It was 7:00 on a Sunday morning, and I was miserable. That was the first moment I realized that I didn't party like my friends. They had a higher tolerance for drinking. They could socialize and laugh and look like they were enjoying it. I was struggling. Outside the bathroom door was a room full of my girlfriends, sleeping off the night before, resting to prepare for the week ahead. Not me. In my mind, I was alone in my misery.

I quit laughing and having fun with my friends.
I stopped going out on the dance floor. I went from an
all-American girl and a social butterfly with an amazing
future to a woman who suffered with anxiety.

I went from enjoying social activities to wanting to disappear and die. I remember walking into a T.G.I. Friday's for dinner with my girlfriends. Because I worked at a Top 40 radio station, I was still incredibly popular, and I would get stopped along the way to my table. I used to relish in the attention. I was a local celebrity. Yet, at one point, I remember thinking, *I just wish I could get from the door to the table without anyone knowing me.* Being popular and trendy contrasted my deteriorating state of being. I was embarrassed, and my inner struggle and outer appearance began to look the same. Acquaintances began asking if I was sick. I was leading a double life. My conscience was continually reminding me of the gap between my portrayal and my reality.

Often, I wondered if there was anyone who would understand
my deepest concerns and have compassion for my challenges,
instead of contempt.

THE
Darkness
GROWS

"Be Kind for everyone you meet is fighting some kind of battle."

—IAN MACLAREN

Chapter Six

After breaking off my engagement to Mitch, I decided that living with four of my party friends was a fantastic idea.

Prior to my big job at the Top 40 radio station, I worked at Dekko's Night Club, an Orlando hotspot open seven nights a week. It was my job to book the entertainment, entertain the celebrities, write the radio commercials, and design billboards to promote the business. Unlike so many other graduates, I really was putting my marketing degree to good use. It was a very high-profile position, and I was honored to be part of the dream team representing Orlando's most popular entertainment venue.

My boss, Mark, owned the club but worked as a criminal defense lawyer during the day. He taught me many lessons about running a business and was incredibly particular about details. I became a valuable member of the team, but my occasional use wasn't escaping notice. One day Mark pulled me aside and said, "Look, I can't really put my finger on all of it, but I know something's going on. Let me buy you one visit with this lady." He handed me the card of a therapist named Sally.

I went to see Sally and was appalled and insulted the first time she labeled me an addict. I had seen addicts on the street and was nothing like those sad losers. An alcoholic or drug addict was dirty, homeless, and lived under a bridge, while I was a pretty blonde, a college-educated woman with an impressive job. I realize looking back now how hypocritical these thoughts were and how this kind of hypocrisy can keep you stuck. Thankfully, Sally was relentless, not letting me hide behind my façade. She taught me to look for similarities of other people suffering from the same illness. Sally was the first person who ever told me that I would die from addiction if I didn't get treatment. I was shocked. She shared a common phrase used among those in recovery that I found to be truthful — addiction inevitably leads to "jails, institutions and death." We spent more time together in the months that followed. She was a tiny brunette with a huge commitment to truth. Sally would remind me, "Anything you place before your recovery, you will lose." Sadly, I did not realize how prophetic Sally's warning would be over my life.

I think the first time my parents had a clue about my problem was when my mom stepped through the front door of my condo one afternoon without an invitation, and I didn't welcome her with open arms like I usually did. We had family in town visiting from Chicago. While my relatives chatted with each other downstairs in my living room, I was up in my bedroom, fearful, and out of my right mind.

My mom and my cousin said, "Come downstairs, Mary Katherine. Don't you want to have lunch with us?" I couldn't get myself out of the room. I responded, "I will meet up with you all later." Soon the front door opened, and they left my home. I could hear them giggle and chatter as they walked down the outside corridor towards the stairway to the car. Sadness filled my soul. Eventually, their voices faded, and silence filled my bedroom. I never made it out of my condo that day. I sat undisturbed in a lonely world of addiction, wondering when they would come back knocking at my door. They never did.

My mom weighs in:

Even during those darkest times, Mary Katherine managed to hold wonderful jobs. But she began disappearing for longer periods of time, which was so unlike her. She loves being around family and friends. She's a social butterfly.

She was nominated as one of the top twenty eligible bachelorettes. She was recognized in the Orlando Sentinel and featured in local magazines for her contributions to the community. I mean, amazing stuff. She was scheduled to go on stage where they were doing fundraising, auctioning off dates with these beautiful bachelorettes for a charity. It was a huge event, and Mary Katherine didn't go! I had no idea why, but I was starting to suspect that alcohol and maybe other substances were the reason.

I had originally intended to go to the charity event, of course. It was an honor, and I was hugely flattered to be part of it. But I drank that evening and didn't show up for the auction, because I was too intoxicated. My parents were there in the crowd wondering why their daughter wasn't coming out on stage. I knew in the weeks leading up to this staged and televised event that I wouldn't be able to pull off such a high-profile nomination. Trying on my beautifully designed tea-length, hot pink strapless dress in the days prior to the media interview, I planned how I would escape the performance. As I stood in the mirror watching my designer make alterations to the dress, I would admire his work, while deep down, I was terrified. The story of unworthiness echoed in my mind. I was dying, and no one even knew it. Would my heart fail today? Yet, I smiled approvingly as he made the changes.

The irony is there *was* a side of me that was an accomplished, talented, community-driven bachelorette up to the call of being nominated. However, there was also a darker side of my image hiding behind the smiles, struggling to stay connected to family and friends. My prophecy fulfilled itself; I called the event director and told him I was very ill with a virus. He was disappointed and surprised, of course. Looking back just days after the fiasco, I deeply regretted my behavior, resenting who I was becoming despite my dreams of being useful in the community and successful in my field.

I was down to ninety-eight pounds. Living a lie was becoming more and more challenging due to my physical appearance, and I knew it was time to finally admit what was going on.

Driving to my parents' house on a Saturday afternoon, I tried to think of ways to break the news to them. There was no positive spin I could put on the facts, so after a nice lunch of chicken pesto, I just put it out there, bluntly, "Mom, Dad, I think I have a drug problem."

Surprisingly, they just kind of shrugged it off. No tears. No drama. It wasn't the reaction I expected. I remember my dad got up from the table and walked into the kitchen as though he missed the entire sentence. My dad said something to the effect of, "Well, don't do it anymore."

He shares his memory:

I didn't know how to respond. That was one of my mistakes, in retrospect. I wish I had done something then. I wish I had said, 'Okay, you're going in for treatment.' I know my response was less than adequate.

Later, Sandy and I talked about that conversation, and it was like we didn't even hear it. It seems silly when you talk about it now. When Mary Katherine got even sicker, I thought, 'How could I have been so stupid to not do anything at the time she told us?'

With what felt like a lack of concern from my parents, I shrugged it off. Maybe I was making a bigger deal of it than it was. Maybe my dad was right – I could quit partying when I wanted to, easy as that.

So, that night I spent time with friends at a local club where we stood shoulder-to-shoulder among strangers who were also looking for a good time. In public, I smiled. Yet, I felt alone in the world that night after such a dry and unfulfilling conversation with my parents. I had a few drinks that night, but I didn't have the desire to use.

I did have the desire to fade away into the background, never to be seen again. Maybe God will take me to heaven while I sleep, so my misery would be over.

Chapter Seven

Once I reached my late twenties, I only attended church on religious holidays but spent hours and hours writing to God in my journals about my deadly vice and the grip it had on me. I knew I was an addict. My therapist, Sally, convinced me of that. But I had no idea how to fix it. Society's pressure for perfection and the stigma of being a young woman addicted to pills was going to steal my joy and threaten my life.

Through writing, I kept reaching out to God. I loved Him. I kept going back in my memory to childhood, recalling how much I adored Jesus and how I prayed He would sit on my bed and listen to my inner struggles.

It occurred to me that maybe I could find help for my anxiety and addiction if I went back to church. Through mutual friends, I met a girl named Liz, who invited me to a Community Church, a nondenominational fellowship in Orlando. It was my first charismatic experience, and I immediately took to the worship music and the Pastor's messages. I began attending two or three services a month and always ended up crying. Yet, even though the sermons were compelling, my physical cravings and anxiety exerted a stronger pull.

I couldn't quit using. I waved my hands and sang along to the praise music, really trying to enjoy those beautiful times at church. But I knew when the service was over, I would cave in order to relieve the cravings.

When Liz moved, I kept going to this church, even taking a few friends along with me. I often got high on a Saturday night, then went to church (still high) on Sunday morning. I switched, then, to a Saturday afternoon service so I could focus on the sermon. Sounds crazy, right? But, I desperately wanted to get well and be happy, joyous and free.

I sat in the back of the church, where it was easier to cry without being noticed. I would listen to the message and agree with everything the Pastor said, but it was like a flesh-versus-spirit thing. My spirit knew that what I was doing was unhealthy, wrong and dangerous, but I couldn't stop. Ironically, the church was only a few blocks from my dealer's house in "the 'hood." Because I was in the fight of my life, I went to church expecting a supernatural healing. When God didn't deliver my healing each week, I was tempted to choose drinking over sobriety. It felt like a tug-of-war inside me, pulling in each direction: life versus death. I was growing resentful of this God who knew I was desperate for a miracle and still wasn't performing like the Pastor promised He could. My prayers weren't being answered. I felt like the Holy Spirit had turned His back on me. I would have months of freedom where I re-gained momentum in my career and relationships, followed by a relapse.

I didn't want to be so sick. I wanted to be in a great relationship, and have kids, and a terrific job, and a stellar relationship with my family. I wanted to experience the kind of contentment and happiness I saw friends enjoying. I didn't want to fear what kind of trouble my Saturday nights would bring after leaving the safety of God's house.

I had gone from a happy-go-lucky young woman to a woman who always felt alone in my much deeper, darker addiction to heavier substances.

By now, I was a burden to anyone who loved me or cared about me. I was stealing their peace of mind. I was not able to show up for my job and constantly called in sick to work. I was unable to show up for family gatherings. The contrast between whom I dreamed of becoming as a little girl and who I became was so drastic that I could hardly wake up each morning, open my eyes, lift myself off the pillow, and start my day. I would look in the mirror and ask myself, *Mary Katherine, how did you get to this point?*

One night I began to fear I would die. I thought, *if my family gets a call that I've passed away, would they ever know how much I loved them?* I wanted them to understand that even in my toughest days alone, I thought about them all the time.

This letter was written when it was the quietest in the wee hours after midnight. That was the time of day I hated the most. I turned on the TV to fill the silence. I drank a cold beer while I wrote this suicide note, taking deep breaths to calm my nerves.

Dear family,

A sudden urge came over me as I was lying down. Because I am an addict who has had a difficult time staying sober, there is always a chance that my heart will decide it's had enough. If you find this, I am with Jesus creating each sunrise and sunset for you to remember me by.

I've tried so many times to get my life back on track. I've just grown tired, so very tired of fighting this intense craving. It's hard to explain the emptiness I feel. My addiction has taken all my God-gifted passions to the point I feel nothing, really, except fear! I feel a lot of that.

You have walked through my journey with me. I just needed to tell you all how much I love you and how grateful I am for all your love, prayers, and commitment to my life. I hope you never see this letter, but I couldn't leave without saying, "I'll see you in Heaven!"

Please forgive me for stealing your peace of mind and causing you pain and worry.

I love you so much,

Mary Katherine

HITTING
ROCK
Bottom

"Hitting rock bottom has the power to springboard you towards freedom."

—MARY KATHERINE MORALES

Chapter Eight

For my job at Dekko's Night Club, I threw a big party with a thousand guests when the club partnered with an adult contemporary radio station that played Top 40 hits. A woman from the station saw the work I was doing and was impressed by my salesmanship and marketing ideas. She pulled me aside one day and said, "If you ever want to get out of this and come to work with me, let me know." Two weeks later, I started working in radio sales with Linda. I left Dekko's so easily, because Linda was a remarkable businesswoman — and I wanted a new career.

I excelled at selling radio ads, hunting down some of the biggest and most prestigious accounts in Orlando. Besides the money, which was three times more than I was making at Dekko's, there were other perks to my new job. I was like a little girl in a candy store, getting all the free tickets to the hottest events. Want to go to the sold-out Janet Jackson concert? I was your girl. Need a free pass to Disney World, or exclusive VIP tickets to a private club? I got it without even breaking a nail. I was the girl who could get you in anywhere. All the velvet ropes lifted when I arrived on the scene.

I set up promotions for a lot of huge concerts: The Dave Matthews Band, C+C Music Factory, The Real McCoy, Fiona Apple, Cheryl Crow, and Hootie and the Blowfish, to name a few. I worked with Shaquille O'Neal and Snoop Dogg when they shot music videos in town. I worked with these celebrities and many more, maintaining a professional façade at work by creating dynamic events, exceeding my sales goals, and establishing strong clientele relationships. My old party friends, however, still sensed that my personal life was spiraling. One night I shared a drink with Allison. She was blunt. "Mary Katherine, you are way too thin. I'm really worried about you. I think you need some help." The absurdity of her confrontation struck me. Allison was the catalyst who introduced me to the nine party girls, putting me on the road to addiction in the first place. But unlike me, Allison controlled her habit. I was barely able to keep my destructive personal life from seeping into my professional one.

My job did nothing to curb my habit. Like many other people, I worked 9 to 5, but my hours were 9:00 p.m. to 5:00 a.m., and my office was whatever bar, club, or concert my client's heart desired. I was getting paid to book advertising, attend parties and entertain celebrities.

I got my stash at an upscale hair salon. I walked in, got my hair done for Saturday night, and exchanged cash for pills in the stock room. I still existed in a world where people drove Lexus cars and lived in beautiful homes on gorgeous Florida waterfronts.

Over time, my frail composure became apparent to my new bosses. Called into the office, my employers told me they didn't want me doing nightclub events anymore because they thought I was burning the candle at both ends. They could see I was getting into trouble doing those events. "You'll keep all the big accounts, like Disney and Blockbuster, but maybe you shouldn't have to go to all these gigs."

They all chose their words carefully, but I knew they were onto my shameful secrets. I was losing control of my behavior. I was becoming more unpredictable. I had lost a tremendous amount of weight, and my "All-American" style was diminishing. I could no longer live two lives.

Chapter Nine

Just like so many of the chapters of my life, this one begins with a man.

Jake was one of the best things to happen to me for a while. He was a handsome, six-foot-three volleyball player with brown hair, blue eyes, and a brilliant mind. He loved music, motorcycles, and politics, yet was soft-spoken. Despite my "issues," we had a healthy relationship. He kept me as grounded as possible and left me in good spirits. Jake showed me what living a clean life could be like.

We met at a trendy nightclub. After exchanging glances all night, he finally walked up to me and asked me to dance. We enjoyed the evening getting to know one another. At closing, he took my number.

Once we celebrated a year of dating, we moved in together. Jake had a great job in pharmaceuticals *(the irony)*, and we spent picture-perfect weekends going motorcycle riding, inviting friends over to the pool, playing volleyball, barbecuing and taking out the wave runners.

I felt rather free. I was hanging out with healthy people. Jake only drank beer, and my alcohol consumption was at a minimum. For two years, I was healthy.

That spring, we went on a fantastic skiing trip in Colorado. It felt so good to get out of Central Florida with Jake and his childhood friends to a place where nobody knew me. I felt a sense of freedom — and a new beginning.

When I was with Jake, I felt healthier, safer, and more protected than I had in years. But it wasn't all perfect. We had our religious differences. He was Jewish, and I was a Christian. Jake promised his grandfather, a Holocaust survivor, he would carry on the legacy of Judaism. But religious differences were not the issue that drove us apart, rather my substance use disorder was the more pressing issue at hand. A little "E" turned into more partying.

Unfortunately, the habit I naively believed I had "under control" once again reared its ugly head. Hiding my use caused an uncomfortable, haunting tension within my soul that followed me everywhere. I didn't trust myself. I wasn't treating the illness by going to meetings or to therapy. I was using healthy people as a bandage to cover my open wound.

But that bandage was suddenly ripped away when Jake broke up with me. I wish I remembered more about what transpired, but I can only recall that I experienced some kind of spiraling-down episode that ended the relationship. Jake realized the contrast and gap between us were too great. He told me, "I love you, Mary Katherine, and I always will, but I'm scared of your habit. I wish I could help you, but I can't. I just can't." I remember exactly where I was standing inside my parents' home that summer afternoon when Jake said those words. I was devastated — heartbroken over the end of our love affair, and inconsolable about the loss of our friendship. To me, Jake wasn't just my boyfriend, he was my best friend. It's probably one of the greatest friendship losses I have ever suffered. He was such a beautiful human being.

I moved back into the safety of my parents' house but soon began hanging out with more dangerous people without Jake to anchor me. I wasn't making it to the radio station every day. People at work knew something was terribly wrong and were pulling me aside, coaching me on what to tell the boss, trying to save my job — and me. A popular DJ walked me to my car one night and physically shook me, saying, "No more! This is it. No more for you. This is ridiculous. You're a beautiful woman with a bright future. You're gonna kill yourself!"

Though I was holding on by my fingernails to this glamorous, lucrative job, one disastrous gig ended my once promising and illustrious career in radio. I organized celebrity appearances to do promotions, inviting some of our biggest clients (mainly Disney and Miller Brewing Company) to meet-and-greet the talent. A lot was riding on the success of this event, not only my job and professional reputation, but hundreds of thousands of dollars in advertising for our station.

Yet, there I sat on a tattered green couch, already an hour late for the event. My so-called friends reminded me that if I made a phone call and spent my last $100, the career I loved would be over. I picked up my cell phone anyway and placed an order for delivery. Looking back, I didn't feel regret about the inevitable loss of my job, but rather an overwhelming sense of relief. My exhausting charade was over.

The night I didn't show up at the event, I left one of my co-workers to entertain my professional guests. Of course, my boss called my cell phone. When I didn't answer, she called my mom and asked if I was on my way.

"I'm not sure," my mom said.

"It's over for Mary Katherine. I love her like a daughter, but I cannot predict her behavior." was my boss's reply before she hung up.

I had lost my $80,000-a-year job, my exciting career, and my VIP status. Oddly, I felt free.

I was so glad I didn't have to fake it anymore. No more getting dressed in the morning, putting on a suit, driving a fancy car, pretending I was okay while privately fighting a battle with substance use disorder and the spirit of fear at night. It was a relief to just be me and not have to pretend to be something I wasn't. I became a woman desperately searching for the love of God to heal me.

THE CLASH BETWEEN

Unworthiness

EVIL AND THE

PROMISES
OF GOD

"Fear not, for I am with you; do not be dismayed, for I am your God; I will stregthen you, I will help you, I will uphold you with my righteous hand,"

(ISAIAH 41:10)

Chapter Ten

THE CLASH BETWEEN UNWORTHINESS, EVIL AND THE PROMISES OF GOD

Eric, who lived near the church I once attended, was my dealer. He was protective of me — as protective as he could be. Because he didn't want to see me in the more dangerous neighborhoods, I went directly to his house. Sometimes, he and his girlfriend let me stay at their place because they were worried about me. He was looking at a once upper-middle-class, college-educated, successfully employed former Homecoming Queen who was in over her head. He would earnestly plead with me to get help, go home, stop calling, quit knocking on his door, and stay away from the dangerous neighborhoods that produced some of Orlando's most dangerous criminals. Yet, because I was desperate to stay on the destructive path, he continued to supply me with the substances of choice. His girlfriend, Mauve, would quietly pull me aside to share her concerns that one day I would die of an overdose, or that I would be a victim in a crime. Yet, I ignored her genuine desire to help me see the truth about myself and the grave danger I was putting myself in.

One night I drove over to Eric's, but he wasn't home. The backseat of my car was covered with recovery literature and workbooks. I was going to 12-Step meetings, but a meeting is only as good as what you do outside the rooms of the program — and I was still using every day.

Without chemicals in my system, I would withdraw, becoming unstable and insecure. My mind would short circuit, becoming utterly focused on getting more pills. It felt like starvation from food, a deep and consuming hunger, only for a chemical fix. Extreme anxiety would overwhelm my aching body, and panic would overtake my mind. I knew the only way I would feel normal again would be to use again. It is a horrible cycle. Desperate for a fix, I drove to the most notorious neighborhood in Orlando.

I was driving around a bad neighborhood, and eventually, I pulled up to a house where a beautiful black woman was standing in the front door. She had gorgeous long black curly hair, loosely hanging around her shoulders and pearly white teeth. Though she was plainly dressed in low-riding jeans and a simple white T-shirt, her outer beauty invited me to trust her immediately. "Hi," I leaned out my car window and said, "I'm looking for Eric."

She told me he wasn't there, but she would be glad to help me. Tina must have sensed I had some money in my pocket, because she invited me to come in for a while and party. I knew better than to go inside, but I did it anyway.

For a half-hour or so, things were fine. She invited me into a room, locked the door behind me, and we sat cross-legged on the floor facing one another while we talked. Without asking me for money, we partied for a while and made small talk. I felt relatively safe at that time. Then, Tina asked if she could borrow my car to go find some more drugs. I hesitated, and that's when the violence began. Tina went crazy. She was a lot bigger than me, as I stood 5 feet 2 inches and weighed 110 pounds while she was at least 5 feet 6 inches and weighed approximately 150 pounds. I could feel her strength as she threw me up against a wall, banging my head against a large framed picture. Before I could catch my breath and figure out what just happened, Tina pinned my shoulders against the wall, thrusting her knee into my stomach, making it clear she was taking my car. Grabbing me by the neck, she pulled me down the hall and threw me into a disgusting hole of a room.

Even in the dark, it was obvious someone lived in the room and was gone at the moment. There was an unmade single bed, and a mangy nightstand topped with an old-fashioned lamp muted by the towel covering its shade. Along the bare wall, a beat-up old dresser missing most of its knobs filled the empty space. As I frantically looked around, I heard her lock the bedroom door – from the outside. Terrified, I knew my life was radically different than it had been just one hour earlier. Frightened to make any movements or sound, I quietly adjusted the curtains on the long horizontal window to shed moonlight into the room in which I was now a prisoner. The view was of a small backyard with rusted patio furniture, overgrown shrubs infested by weeds and a porch without screens. I searched hysterically for the face of a neighbor; there was no one to help me in this direction. I tried to open the window to escape, but it was either painted or nailed shut.

I looked around the room. Dirty clothes were thrown on the floor, along with old food wrappers, which smelled like bitter fruit. The green carpet was worn and dirty. I quietly sat on the floor, knees to chest, head down, leaning against the bed, praying for God to spare me harm, and take me home. I begged forgiveness, as I promised to get help and never return to this neighborhood. I felt a moment of relief, but help never came.

Before Tina took off, she barged into the bedroom, dragged me out, and made me sign a makeshift contract stating I allowed her to use my car. Tina gave strict instructions to the others in the living room to prevent me from leaving or making any contact with my family. She snatched up my keys before locking us all inside the house.

There were four of us. Thomas, a mahogany-colored man in his fifties who looked damaged from years of addiction and the hard work needed to support his habit. Surprisingly, he was a gentle man, soft-spoken with a lean body and a simple smile. His wife, Linda, a white woman in her late forties, was weirdly out of place in this house. She, too, was unusually soft-spoken, but she seemed balanced and happy to live in such squalor. Jackson, in his late twenties, must have been a remarkable little boy. In spite of being locked in this crazy house, he was polite and had a confident demeanor.

> *Little did I know that each of these three strangers would one day be remembered as heroes.*

I wondered how they had gotten into this dark, roach-infested predicament. Perhaps the same way I did — one bad decision at a time.

For the next five days, I was held prisoner – locked inside this house with these strangers and kept alone in the bedroom much of the time, while Tina used my car. I wasn't allowed to leave the room other than to use the restroom or get a glass of water. Starving without food, a woman assigned to watch over me gave me a piece of her fried chicken. I ate with determination, because I didn't know if I would ever eat again. Crying out loud, I begged and begged for someone to let me go home. I wanted my cell phone back. I wanted so badly to get word to my parents or my brother that I was alive. For hours, I sat imagining the grief and sorrow my family was feeling since my disappearance. I would daydream about what I would say to my mom and dad if I ever got to see them again. I would kneel against the bed, praying for God to save me.

Sitting in my "prison cell" of a bedroom, I was on a crazy mind trip. Tina would pull up in my car, drop off a handful of pills, and I would stay continually stoned. Yet even though I was heartbroken and paranoid, I tried to focus on the fact that I had guardian angels protecting me. I prayed to God for help and tried to thank him for keeping me alive long enough to turn 30 years old.

Word got around that I was in the house. Eric had a cousin named Rodney to whom I owed $50. When Rodney learned I was at Tina's place, he came over and began pounding on the front door. I couldn't open it, because I had been locked in from the outside.

"You're in my neighborhood now, bitch!" he screamed, adding plenty of vulgar and colorful words. "I want my fifty bucks you white, snobby bitch. You'd better find a way to get me my money, or I will kill your fucking ass."

Petrified, I answered through the door, "As soon as Tina lets me out of this house, I'll find my bank card and get you the money."

Rodney tried to kick the front door in but was unsuccessful. That only enraged him more. He wanted his money and decided to rile up the neighborhood. At this point, the three strangers transferred me from the room facing the back of the house to Thomas's room near the front of the house. His room was bare, with old terrazzo floors that stayed cool to the touch. There was a simply decorated queen-sized bed he shared with Linda, and a cheap abstract framed picture from the Seventies above it. They had a small white refrigerator along a wall, with two chairs and a table supporting a toaster and coffee maker. There was a wooden ledge they used for storing groceries and personal hygiene products. A television perched on another bookshelf with other knickknacks. Their closet was full of clothes, scrapbooks, and a stack of old record albums almost five feet tall. I could tell this small room inside the drug house was their private world. Somehow, they had made this awful place a "home." Linda was inside the room, propped up on her bed smoking dope and watching television, when Thomas and Jackson hurried me across the hall and inside this new hideout.

A huge crowd grew outside the window, getting louder and louder. "I'll shoot her upside the head," I heard Rodney boast. Faceless men standing outside the window began to make threats against my life, all over $50. I heard fierce voices threatening to rape me. They would laugh and describe how they would prove that a rich white girl couldn't come into their neighborhood, steal from a black man, and get away with it. As others joined the group outside, and I heard them plan how they would kill me, I began to sob uncontrollably. I knew that I was in grave danger; I had crossed into a world of street politics and hood power plays that I didn't understand and could not control. The mob of men cheered and began banging on the window, trying to break it. They moved from window to window, trying to find out where I was hiding. They came to the front door, hammering and beating on it to gain entrance into the house, where room by room they planned to hunt me down. These were gang members and criminals ready to back up their boy, wronged, and in their minds disrespected, by this rich white chick.

I cowered in the closet, hiding behind the stacked records, praying and trying to make a deal with God. My blood pressure soared, as I envisioned a dozen men breaking down the bedroom door, pulling me out of the closet, raping and beating me until I was totally broken. Then, once I was totally violated, they would kill me. I visualized my mom and dad crying over the loss of their once-beautiful daughter. I was heartbroken, horrified, and terrified as I heard my name chanted outside the feeble walls. Through the windows, they would say, "Mary Katherine, we are coming in. Mary Katherine, we are coming to find you." One guy kept making comments about wanting to harm me to teach me a lesson for not paying Rodney back.

Thomas must have grown tired of the escalating riot, because he ran outside and tried to calm everyone. It didn't work. Through the window, I heard a huge fight break out. The sudden sounds reminded me of a lion pride fighting over the recent kill. Roars of anger came from some men with louder voices who shouted obscene words while others banged on the window with pieces of rebar. I heard others, who perhaps were the weaker members, fighting off to the side of the house. I have no idea what happened exactly, but it must have been terrible. Moments later, miraculously, Thomas managed to get back inside the house, slammed the door, and stumbled through the bedroom doorway. Frozen in horror, I could see his arm was broken in multiple places. His face was beaten with one eye completely shut; his lip was split wide open and bleeding, and his mutilated arm swung off uselessly to his right side. Thomas couldn't control his sobbing due to the pain of his numerous injuries, and he was headed to the hospital. "Mary Katherine, I can't help you anymore," he groaned. "You're on your own. Stay in the closet and don't come out until someone comes to get you." I felt crazed with anger for what they had done to him. Yet, I was powerless and still in severe danger.

Tina suddenly pulled up in the driveway in my car. She rushed into the house and began planning the escape to take Thomas to the hospital. Frantically, I pleaded with Tina, "Please don't leave me here alone. I promise to stay low in the backseat. Just drop me off somewhere, and I promise not to tell anyone. Please take me with you to the hospital. If you leave me here, they will kill me." Tina shrugged me off, demanding I stay behind. She assigned the woman who walked into the house with her to stay behind with me. As I perched to look outside the window, I watched Tina pay Rodney the $50. I heard her shouting at the men outside that if anyone so much as put one finger on me, they'd have a huge debt to pay. As Tina pulled away with Thomas in my car, the noise and the threats on my life began again. I felt like my very life was rolling away with my now beat-up car. This time, the mob was louder and more destructive, breaking glass, banging iron rods against one another, and destroying the outside patio furniture. The front door became a pounding drum; they were trying to beat the door down.

I cowered behind any junk I could find in the closet, envisioning the local news report that there had been a brutal gang rape and murder of one of the "twenty most eligible bachelorettes" in Orlando. I saw the funeral procession, the hearse, and tears on the faces of my family. I begged God to keep me from dying this way. I wanted to make things right with my mom. My heart was beating so fast that I prayed I would die of a heart attack rather than what I knew was coming.

Jackson, the young black man from across the hall, walked in the room, grabbed my hand, and lifted me out of the closet. He said, "Lady, calm down, or you will have a heart attack and die. You've got to breathe. You are in serious trouble, but you have got to keep your head about you right now."

Strangely, we sat on the edge of the bed, and he held my hands to comfort me, careful not to move or speak so that no one outside would hear us and know what room I was in. Once I caught my breath, the woman Tina assigned to watch over me came in, grabbed my wrist, and took me to the original bedroom – Tina's room – where this nightmare began. The thumping on the swing-away bars hinged to the windows continued for hours while the violent men lingered outside. My large female "bodyguard" offered me more drugs to keep me prisoner in mind and body. I declined the offer, despite my desire to escape. The sounds moved from the front of the house to the side where I was hiding. I ached with sadness. As I heard voices move near the window, I slid behind the eight-foot armoire in Tina's room and hunched in the corner, so no one could see me through the blinds. Terrified, I stayed there, and the so-called bodyguard eventually left me there to fend for myself. I remained in the corner, in tears and dog-tired from the hours of off-and-on window banging. Hours later, Thomas and Linda returned from the hospital. I demanded to know, "Where is Tina? Why is she leaving me here to die?" Neither Thomas nor Linda replied.

Now in the wee hours of the morning, the noise outside ceased, and I begged Thomas to allow me to sleep on their cold, damp floor. I promised not to move, speak, or cause any trouble. They must have known I was still in unbelievable danger. By the grace of God, they showed me kindness by giving me a thin blanket, a tiny white pillow, and a small space at the foot of their queen-sized bed. Lights were out, and I could hear Thomas groaning in pain. My heart broke as I lay there, helpless. I didn't dare fall asleep for fear someone would break down the bedroom door. It grew eerily quiet, and I lay still, watching the dim lights in the gap under the door. Occasionally, I saw footsteps move along the hallway. No words were spoken. Paralyzed in fear, I'd watch for them to move past the door. I didn't dare breathe as they walked by. Though I will never know who walked through the house later that night, my guess is that it was Jackson and the bodyguard checking on the status inside the house. The Devil himself loves chaos and harm. I truly believe the battle for my life was more spiritual than physical.

I believe the reason the gang outside didn't break in was that my guardian angel, the warrior, stood guard.

Threatening to take my life over 50 bucks isn't rational; though the fighting manifested in the physical realm, it started in the minds of evil men who had lost contact with God.

The next morning was my thirtieth birthday. As I sat up, I realized the riot outside was over. I was in complete shambles, emotionally. I hadn't eaten anything substantive or slept in five days.

Thomas had been my only defender, so I tried to sweet-talk him into letting me go. I offered to send him money once I returned home. I told him it was my birthday and my parents would be looking for me. "Until Tina comes back, you don't leave," he said. I'm sure he was angry that his act of goodwill had gotten him nothing but a broken arm, a black eye, multiple stitches above his upper lip, and an unwanted house guest.

Finally, later that morning, Jackson came home with news that Tina had been busted for selling drugs. There was no reason to keep me anymore. He warned Thomas, "You better get her out of here, because Tina's in jail and they've impounded the white girl's car. The police are driving around the streets now looking for her."

A large group of men I had never seen before arrived shortly after Jackson, and they didn't know what to do with me. If they let me walk out of the house, there was a chance a patrol car would round the corner, and I'd be seen walking out of the place. A blond-haired, green-eyed Caucasian woman would draw the wrong kind of attention. At the same time, no one wanted to stow me away in their vehicle for fear of being caught kidnapping. The men decided the latter was a better option but warned me not to sit up in the back seat of the car. Within minutes, a tall thin stranger, who had never met me before, hurriedly stowed me in his back seat and drove slowly down the street while listening to rap music. I began to fear that he might be taking me to a vague location to "finish me off," since I knew information about Tina, the violence inside the house and the names of those who came and went over the five days I was held prisoner. I was relieved when he dropped me off at a neighborhood gas station. *Exhale. I received a miracle.*

Two minutes later, a patrol car pulled up, and the officer said they had been looking for me. I broke down and sobbed while calling my dad from the officer's phone. The policeman looked at my driver's license and said, "You are beautiful in this picture."

"Thanks," I muttered.

"You're in over your head, young lady. I've worked this neighborhood for years, and you won't resemble this picture in a year, if you keep coming back."

My dad drove up in his brown Mercedes, and we collapsed in each other's arms. I cried, repeating over and over, "I don't want to do this. I don't want to be here anymore. I would rather die."

He remembers:

When I picked her up, she said she was done. She looked like hell. To this day, I still don't know what went on those five days she was held hostage. I don't know if I want to ever know.

Dad took me to the hospital, but they wouldn't admit me. Detoxing from a chemical dependency is more of a physical breakdown than detoxification from alcohol. Mom got on the phone and agreed to look for a treatment facility. She found a place called *Alternatives in Treatments*, three hours away in West Palm Beach.

My mom eventually arrived, and she ran to the car to see me through the window. Aghast, she backed away. By now, my eyes were barely open from hunger, fatigue, and post-traumatic stress. Black and blue bruises covered my legs, arms and shoulders. Both my mom and I silently agreed we didn't have the strength in that moment to embrace once another. We were both hardly able to conceive our reality. Without a word, she placed her hand on the glass of the passenger's window, began to cry, and stepped back from me. I, too, began to weep inside the car, knowing exactly what she was thinking, but grateful to be alive. Mom met Dad in the parking lot of the hospital, and they talked about me as if I wasn't there. I wasn't allowed to speak as I sat in the back seat. It was like I was a child all over again – and I was. My life choices had gotten me to the point where I was incapable of taking care of myself. I needed my parents to make the decisions for me.

"I cannot handle her," my mother said. "This is too dangerous. She needs to be someplace where someone professional can help her."

She picks up the story later in my transition to the treatment center:

Mary Katherine was out cold, just done. Passed out. She had barely survived being kidnapped and was lucky to be alive. I sat in the back seat with her head in my lap on the way to West Palm Beach. She slept from the time we packed her bags to the moment we arrived.

I remember the snapshot they took of her at the treatment center. Her hair was pulled straight back, and it was filthy dirty. Her skin was gray and looked old and haggard. Leaving her there was the toughest thing we had ever done.

When it was time to write the check, we found out the bill came to nearly the same amount John and I had received in the mail that day. Praise God!

My dad continues:

We didn't have extra money because we had just opened a business and were struggling. I had just received a check that day for a house closing for thirty-six hundred dollars and had just deposited it.

The first payment for Mary Katherine's treatment was thirty-three hundred dollars. I told Sandy, "God works in mysterious ways." The fact that he had provided was a divine-guided intercession. He knew we needed that money to get our girl the medical and mental help she needed.

Being checked into the rehab center on my thirtieth birthday was heart-wrenching for me. We arrived at the treatment center around 10:00 p.m. I felt completely wiped out, and I could barely stand. I vaguely remember getting out of the car, grabbing my purse in search of makeup to cover up the emotional scars of my last five days. Furious, my dad yelled, "What in the hell are you doing, Mary Katherine? No amount of makeup will cover your mistakes!" He was correct. And the sad thing is that I would even give a thought to outer appearances, with utter chaos happening on the inside. I didn't know what city I was in or where they had taken me. I thought, will I ever go home again? I walked into what appeared to be the check-in area, where they took my photograph, my blood pressure, and asked us basic questions. Molly and Dove checked me in that night. I will always remember them for their kindness and compassion.

My parents and I embraced one last time, as though saying goodbye forever. It was incredibly hard to watch them leave the facility, not knowing when I would see them. They had been my lifeline and my prayer warriors for several years. As my parents left me behind, I walked into a room full of addicts who welcomed me to the facility. I remember all sorts of men and women sitting on a couch inside the main television area, laughing as they watched a movie. I felt as though I was in a time warp. Only 12 hours earlier, I had been in a life-threatening situation surrounded by violence and drug dealers, and I couldn't comprehend what was happening. Who were these smiling faces? I hadn't laughed or smiled in a long time. What impact would they have in my life?

Moments later, I was escorted to a bedroom just off to the right of the manager's office, where I changed into pajamas. Only a dim light lit the room, and there were two neatly made twin beds that lined the wall. Though I didn't know where I was, I knew I was finally safe and in good hands. I slept for two days, interrupted only when the patient techs checked to see if I was breathing. Though I had major bruises on my legs and arms from being pulled around and shoved into different rooms, my physical injuries were minor. The lump on the back of my head from Tina shoving me into the wall had disappeared. The patient techs would take my temperature, and to prevent dehydration, they would ask me to sit up to drink water throughout my 48 hours of sleep. On the third day, a tall, lean woman named Doreen nudged me until I was coherent. She gave me orders to get up, eat, and get ready to attend a meeting. I stumbled around the dim room, trying to acclimate to my surroundings. Still unaware of exactly where I was, I put on my blue jeans, a yellow tank top and flip flops.

Others were eating in the common area, but I was unable to eat. We loaded into a big white van and traveled to a meeting hall. As I sat outside of the Recovery clubhouse, a woman named Shannon came to me, smiled, and shook my hand. She was the first normal-looking person I had seen in months.

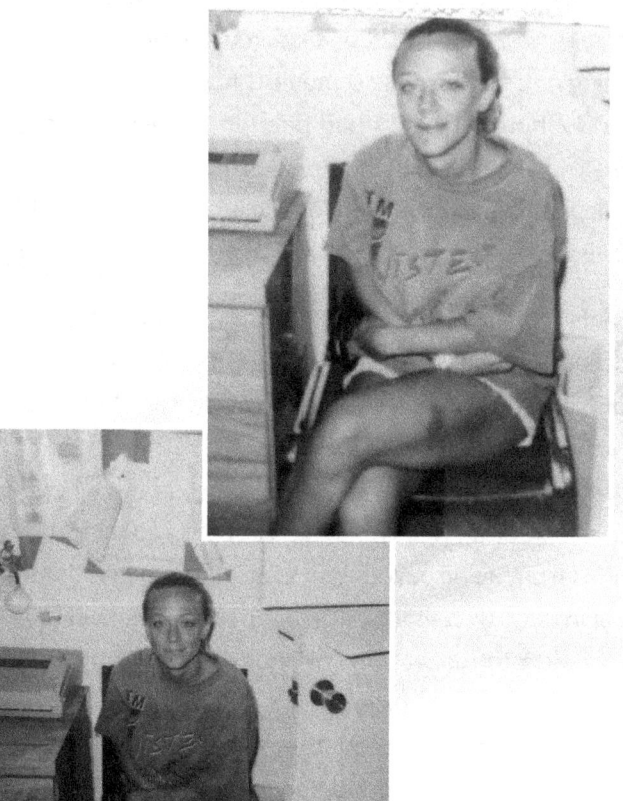

September, 4,1999. Being admitted to a trauma and treatment center, Delray Beach, FL. Exhausted, but relieved to be in a safe place. I will always be thankful to Molly and Dove who served as the medical technicians that evening.

THE *Journney* HOME BEGINS

"*My darling, no matter what the enemy whispers;*
you are never alone. The Holy Spirit is
always with you."

—MARY KATHERINE MORALES

Chapter Eleven

Inside the rehab center, I received a letter from my mom.

It read:

Dearest Mary Katherine,

Remember when no one else believed you could compete on the swim team because of your serious ear problems? You found a way to not just be on the team but to be number one. Remember when you wanted to be a cheerleader, but hundreds of girls tried out for the few spots? You found a way to win your spot and earn All American Cheerleader, too.

Remember when your grades said "junior college," but your heart said "university"? You found a way to go to UCF as a cheerleader, join Zeta, Little Sister, O-Team, and on and on and on, all the way to graduation day.

Mary Katherine, there is great power in making a commitment to bettering your life. You have proven that in so many ways, and on so many days.

You will find your way now, because you never give up, you never give in, and you never walk alone. I believe in you!

Love, Mom XO

I, in turn, began to journal my own thoughts:

Tonight, I sit outside for the first time in months, appreciating the night air and smell of the trees and the surroundings. However, I feel very depressed and alone. My mind tells me I should just give up and continue on the journey to the bottom. But the few memories I have tell me to run toward the light of the Lord and hold on.

Why isn't a sale of $3 million for my company more gratifying? When did I decide that a night out with my friends partying would be more worthwhile than time with a significant other or my family? When did I begin choosing pain over joy?

I keep flashing back to winning Homecoming Queen for Lake Brantley High School. I was focused on the one or two people out there who didn't want me to win. Where did I learn all that shame, guilt, and fear?

Allison, my best friend, once told me I was really hard to get close to. I was shocked! She and I shared everything, so I thought. But really, she had shared, and I had listened. When I was hurting or suffering, I simply hid my emotions by smiling and pretending I was okay.

Now I'm at the point where hiding doesn't work. I'm not that good an actress. My face and eyes show that I am not a happy young woman. I've been taught by my parents, teachers, and role models that people don't like people who don't have it all together. In order to have lots of friends and respect from your peers, people learn to hide their shortcomings and only share the 'good' things in life.

Now, I think the only way to have true friends is to be myself. I need to allow myself to be vulnerable and tell the ones I love that I am hurting.

After two months of rehab, I did meet someone who would become a true friend for the rest of my life. I stood in church on a Wednesday night and sang the praise choruses up on the overhead screens. There was a woman standing on stage on the worship team who kept glancing at me, and we continued making eye contact until the end of the song.

When the pastor invited everyone in the auditorium to walk around and introduce themselves, I thought to myself, *I'm gonna go shake that woman's hand.* I headed to the base of the stage and extended my arm.

"I'm Mary Katherine."

"Karla, nice to meet you."

I had been praying for female friends. I was lonely, and my heart yearned for a sister in Christ who had what I wanted and could bring out the best in me.

Karla's take:

From the stage view, I could see her sitting in the audience. I'd never seen her before, but I thought, "Gosh, she just looks like a sunflower." She had long, curly, blonde hair, and I thought to myself that I'd really like to get to know her. When it was time to shake hands, she walked down to the stage and shook mine. I thought that was unusual. Generally, people in the crowd didn't approach the platform.

From there, we started connecting. We went to a women's luncheon and became friends. I just thought she was very confident and outgoing. I was divorced and single, and the two of us were in the same boat. I had faced problems in life and was attending recovery meetings for alcohol addiction, but it took a while for Mary Katherine to open up about her drug problems.

One of the things I noticed was that she was very guarded. I wondered why she didn't trust me. She was often very elusive and cold at times, and

I couldn't understand why. I thought she didn't like me or that I wasn't cool enough for her.

She and I attended meetings together, but I never really knew what the truth was with Mary Katherine. I liked her, but she was a tough person to figure out.

THE
HOLY SPIRIT
Speaks
IN MOMENTS OF
DESPAIR

"It takes great courage to stand
where fear once stood."

—MARY KATHERINE MORALES

Chapter Twelve

After hiding away in the rehab center for 45 days, my counselor declared my addiction treatment complete and encouraged me to venture back out in public.

In treatment, I began to reconnect with Jesus, starting with the simple act of kneeling at the end of my bed. With the sun shining through the window and on my face, I would ask every morning, as earnestly as I could muster, for God to fill every fiber, every cell, every muscle of my body with recovery. I begged forgiveness for my sins and shared with Him a desire to change.

I was so vulnerable and broken then — still dealing with post-traumatic stress in the aftermath of being held prisoner and threatened with violence and death for five days, along with all the hurtful memories of loss and pain I caused others.

Therapy was valuable and taught me to empower myself, to see the big picture and have the courage to dream about a life as a Woman of Principle. Working with my therapist was really a new opportunity to practice living an honest life and putting God first.

I wanted so much to be well. One night, I asked myself and God, "How did I get here?" It was a long night of tears. However, I connected with God that night, as I lay crying and meditating on my bed and was Spirit-led to scripture I'd never read before.

Suddenly, without warning, I envisioned myself inside a white cloud, and the Holy Spirit whispered, "This is my beloved Son, in whom I am well pleased. Hear Him!"

I didn't know the significance of the white cloud or the words I heard in the moment. I sat up, went over to my Bible, picked it up and opened the book directly to Matthew 17:5-8.

Remarkably, just like my vision, there was a white cloud described in the verses, just like the one I envisioned surrounding me during my meditation. In this passage, Jesus came to the suffering disciples, touched them, and said, "Arise, and do not be afraid." I was overwhelmed with tears of joy! I was not alone. The Holy Spirit literally comforted me that night. In that moment, I had the courage to rise to a new call upon my life. It was a scripture that I came to lean on during this time. Those passages renewed my inner strength to move forward whenever I became worried or thought I was alone.

I lived with some amazing women for several months. It gave me the chance to gather my strength, build friendships and get back into the workforce.

Karla welcomed me into her home when it was time to move on.

Her words:

When she called me and told me she was looking for an apartment, I told her to come on over. She stayed in my daughter's room and lived with me for six months.

I knew she was lost and hurting. There were a couple times she came into my bedroom in the middle of the night and said, "I'm scared. Can I sleep with you?" I said, "Yeah, get in bed." She was afraid of the dark, of the unknown.

I still didn't know the whole story yet. I didn't fully understand her fears. It wasn't until a couple years later that she started divulging her past. Once she began telling me the stories of her past, then I understood why she was so timid and afraid.

Throughout all the challenges, we developed a strong bond. I knew she was in a spiritual battle, and I didn't want to harbor animosity. I just loved her and continued to pray for her healing.

After leaving Karla's home, I was living in a tiny cottage apartment at the end of a quiet dirt road. I loved that place. Though it was small, it had character. I planted a small garden out front alongside a simple pebbled porch, where I would sit and listen to music. It was one of the gifts I left behind. I had received a big settlement from a car accident, which paid the rent and all my expenses for six months. Now, I had enough money to either start my life in sobriety or really destroy my life.

Luckily, years before I adopted a great, big Rottweiler named Pugsley. I finally found a friend who didn't judge me so harshly. This dog was my lifeline, and I loved her dearly. We did everything together, and she watched over me.

Pugs was my furry guardian angel, and we ate breakfast, lunch, and dinner together. It was almost certain I would get fresh air daily, because she demanded a walk alongside the train tracks where she could run free. I would follow and watch her dash wildly through the fields. This was the only moment of joy I had every day. She loved me no matter what, and I needed that love to stay grounded, even if it came from a dog.

One afternoon as I showered, my heart began to beat very fast, either from fatigue and lack of good food, or strain from all the late nights. Frightened, I stepped out of the water to call for help. As I leaned down and wrapped myself in a towel, Pugs moved in close to me, pushed me to the floor, and laid on my lap to warm me up. She leaned in closely, intuiting I was in some kind of danger. I believe her warmth settled my nerves and prevented me from passing out. That day, she didn't leave my side. Though she seemed upset with me, Pugsley just sat close and watched me. That evening when I got into bed, she hopped up alongside me, lying close as if to guard me. As I drifted off to sleep, I caught her watching me. I will always be grateful for her unconditional love and patience.

As I focused on trying to rebuild my life, I sometimes let my parents down. One Mother's Day weekend, I promised my mom I would come home to Orlando and go out to breakfast at her favorite beachfront restaurant. But I never showed up for her special day. I finally worked up the courage to call her and thought for sure she was just going to be outraged with me.

I'll never forget her words: **"My sweet Mary Katherine would never miss Mother's Day."** She quietly asked me to pack up and come home. Again, she knew that the sober Mary Katherine underneath all this anguish would never miss a holiday with her.

This offering of grace stayed with me forever. In that moment, she created space for me to get well and gave me yet another gift of unconditional love. Despite my outward behavior during my battle with the devil and substance use disorder, my mom knew she will always be my dearest confidant and best friend. Over the years, this example of grace encouraged me to become a Woman of Principle.

Two plus years came and went. I would have incredible year-long periods of sobriety, but then I would crash. I had one foot in the world of recovery and wellness, and one foot in the underground world of alcoholic behavior. I had new friends with fantastic relationships, strong ties in the work community, and respectable lives of service in church and recovery. I met and closely followed a small group of Christian recovering friends. We went to church on Wednesdays, attended inspiring Christian rock concerts, and sang songs of praise to God as we traveled back and forth to the performances. I was deeply grateful not to be alone all the time. When I would fall away for a short time, I would hear a tap on my door late at night, and that same small group would come plead with me to start anew.

We'd sit outside under the stars and share dreams of who we hoped to become. Then we would pray, asking God for strength, so I could place my life firmly in His hands.

I moved into a safe, loving house with a friend in recovery, determined to live abundantly in God's grace and become a Woman of Principle.

Along the way, I landed a job at Houston's, one of the nicer restaurants in the area.

My first day on the job changed my life forever – January 6th. I remember being very nervous as my trainer, Rachel, hovered over my shoulder.

I welcomed a table of ten men and asked for their drink order. The guys began teasing their friend, Al, who was sitting in the corner wearing a white T-shirt emblazoned with a fishing symbol. He seemed shy, and I thought he was kind of cute.

His friends urged him to flirt with my trainer, Rachel. "Forget Rachel, who's the blonde?" he replied.

I blushed and walked away.

Al came in on a regular basis from then on, and he saw to it I was always his server. We engaged in sparkling conversation. Although the flirtation was enjoyable, I tried to make it clear to him I had didn't want to date anyone. The reality was I secretly felt that if he knew the truth about me, he would lose interest. But Al was persistent and kept coming back.

We spoke a few times on the phone before he finally asked me out for the first time, a breakfast date. I previously had such nice cars that I didn't want him to see the simple little Toyota I now drove; it embarrassed me.

I also didn't want him seeing where I lived, since I was rooming with women in recovery. He didn't know my secret yet. The embarrassment over my car and living conditions left me behaving rather elusively, so I arranged to meet him at the restaurant.

Finally, when Al asked me out on our first real evening date, I had to come clean and tell him about my recovery. He didn't flinch; he just came and picked me up. I wasn't sure I wanted to date him, because we seemed so different on the outside. He drove a truck and enjoyed hunting, loved country music, always wore cowboy boots, was a construction superintendent, and was proud to describe himself as an "outdoorsman." I had never met or dated anyone with those interests. I saw myself dating a man who drove a BMW, worked in corporate America, loved social events and dreamed of traveling to exotic places.

However, Al slowly melted my resistance. When I mentioned my favorite musician was Natalie Merchant, that sweet man went to the trouble of calling a radio station and asking, "Who is Natalie Merchant, and where do I get her CDs?" That night, he brought me a CD along with a beautiful white rose from his garden.

He was a very charming, laid-back guy – a true gentleman. We went on six dates before he tried to kiss me goodnight. It had been a long time since I had dated someone as kind as Al. My fear of rejection and my history, however, kept me from fully embracing the connection we had. I promised myself to never give my heart away to another man. Al was a little standoffish, too, probably because he had been burned by a marriage that ended badly.

I didn't mind his caution, because it meant I didn't have to be fully emotionally involved with him. I always had an "out." When making plans with him, I would say, "Okay, let's spend time together until two. But at three o'clock, I have this thing I have to do."

I kept him at arm's length until the day I realized my feelings had changed. After bike riding, we stopped at the health food store, and suddenly it hit me — I didn't want to leave. I didn't need an "out" anymore. I realized I liked Al so much that the spirit of fear was disappearing.

We were driving in his truck one Saturday afternoon when I found myself saying, "I don't really want this date to end." He responded, "Why don't I drop you off, you can get ready, and I can take you to dinner?" Then he smiled.

For the next year, the feelings intensified. We rode bikes, went to the movies, ate at nice restaurants, and took long walks along Delray Beach's Atlantic Avenue, where we shared ice cream and coffee. We laughed a lot, and shared thoughts and ideals and dreams that mattered most to us. We traveled to the Florida Keys and went bike riding along sandy shores. We took his boat out and spent hours wading in the blue waters off Singer Island. We were the picture of romance. We began to open up about our desires and fears. And in the process, we became best friends. I felt great joy and freedom on many days.

Al began to know me for who I was, and he loved all of me. He saw the best in me.

The first truly romantic thing Al said to me was, "I am not sure whose prayers were answered when we met... mine or yours."

I asked myself if this could be real love. I moved again, into an apartment in a beautiful complex with a female roommate, which was another sign of my growth and well-being. When my parents offered me a job with their real estate company, I jumped at the chance to use my marketing skills again, but it meant moving back to Orlando.

Al and I continued to see each other. We didn't want 180 miles of distance between the two cities to stop us, so every weekend one of us drove to see the other.

Eventually, it was time to meet Al's daughter, Mia, a tiny brunette with tons of hair and big brown eyes. I really wanted her to love me because I was falling in love with her dad. I called my best friend, Lynne, and said, "I don't know what to say to this little girl."

"Things will be fine," she reassured me. "She's going to show you her boo-boos, and tell you about school, and say all the things little kids say. Talk to Mia like you talk to your beautiful goddaughters, Madyson and Chloe."

Al and I set up a situation, pretending to accidentally meet while he was spending time with Mia on Singer Island – the accidental/on purpose run-in. It worked like a charm, and Mia, who just turned seven, asked me to join them for dinner. Mia and I sat alongside the ocean seawall, pointing out fish and giggling as the sun set in front of us.

Later, while waiting for the valet to bring around his truck, Al asked Mia, "Hey, do you mind if Mary Katherine rides home with us?"

I nervously stood there while Mia didn't answer her dad. The valet pulled up in the truck. Al looked at me, shrugging, unsure of what to do. But just before Mia climbed in, she tapped me on the arm and said, "Come on. The truck's here. We gotta' go!"

My heart melted when she invited me to come along. We had a good time on the ride home, and that led to a series of meet-ups – going to the movies, nights at the pizza place – activities we could enjoy together. Her sweet nature was another gift God gave me. Without children of my own, I had never really received this kind of love from a child. A child's love is different from the love of an adult, friend or parent. Mia's kindness gave me hope that I could accept love again and trust that I was worthy of an amazing life. Mia taught me to have confidence in intimate, loving relationships. Because she lived with Al, I learned how to care for a child, which included making huge sacrifices. My deep affection for Mia gave me a chance to practice unconditional love for another human being.

As I played the role of a mother, the desire to give her a wonderful life began to transform my heart and soul.

Though Mia and Al became a ray of sunshine in my new life, I couldn't shake the darkness of my old life. I continued to drink sporadically and secretively, fearing Al or Mia might catch on.

Yet, there were plenty of positive experiences, too. I was learning to live one day at a time and be true to myself, grow in my faith and walk confidently among my peers. I created successful radio and media campaigns that generated new business for my parent's company. My dad and I started a charity for children whose parents were in the service defending our country overseas, raising thousands of dollars and getting the local media to adopt the charity. Thousands of toys were donated to support military families. The National Guard gave me a medal of honor. I reconnected with my old friends at the radio station and regained my reputation and popularity.

Then, Al invited me to move in with him and his daughter. We wanted to take our relationship to next level and were tired of the long-distance commute. For Mia's sake, I moved into the guest bedroom.

I added church services back into my life. The first time I attended Al's non-denominational church, I was shocked. Unlike the reserved Catholic Masses I was used to, this was a charismatic fellowship. Catholics never raised their hands or expressed faith in such a magnetic, external way. On my first visit, people spoke in tongues during the service. I sat in the pew, thinking: *What is that? Are people speaking in their native languages?* I just thought it was really odd.

I had never heard praise and worship music like the songs they were singing at Trinity Church. At my church in Orlando, I learned a lot of praise and worship songs, but this was animated gospel music. People waved their hands in the air. A woman next to Al and me clapped her hands and shouted, "Hallelujah, amen!"

It is funny now looking back, but I kept waiting for someone to tell her to be quiet because she was interrupting the service. It was really strange for me, but I grew to love it. I became the woman clapping her hands in the service, giving God all the glory. Trinity was an amazing place filled with diverse cultures and people who had a profound faith in God. This church became my saving grace and the path that led me to a deeper relationship with the Holy Spirit. Trinity Church became our home worship center. It is where I gained a two-year certificate in theology including Old and New Testament studies along with the Study of Faith. This pastoral staff opened the door to supernatural teaching, which changed my life and my understanding of the Holy Spirit forever.

My journey of Becoming a Woman of Principle began to materialize. It was during this time that I developed the courage to live boldly one day at a time. Can you related, beautiful reader? Have you ever overcome a challenging circumstance and come to trust that God would use it for good?

THE
SHARP TEETH
OF
Addiction

"Jesus looked at them and said, "With man all things are impossible, but with God all things are possible."

(MATTHEW 19:26)

Chapter Thirteen

Even though Al and I were happy in our relationship, the sharp teeth of addiction returned and gnawed at my soul. A year of wonderful sobriety, during which I built strong work and family relationships, came crashing down when I succumbed to temptation once more. I was careful to never drink around Mia — at least I knew enough not to inflict my problems on an innocent child.

At times when Al went away on hunting trips, I began checking myself into hotels, such as the Hampton Inn Suites or the Ritz Carlton.

I looked like any other professional businesswoman dressed in a blazer and skirt, rolling my luggage bag into the lobby of a beautifully decorated hotel. But unlike others, inside my suitcase would be a stash of wine, uppers, downers and beer.

After nights like this in my hotel room, my head would clear enough in the morning to write down my thoughts, even do a little poetry writing.

The birds chirping outside the window were a bittersweet sound: It brought the assurance I made it through another long night, but also a sledgehammer of regret that I had wasted another precious day of my life. I tried to make up for it by jotting down my thoughts. I figured that if I wrote a book that helped other people, my life wouldn't have been completely pointless. The fact that I was writing a book about addiction while still drinking was a distinction lost on me at that time.

One morning, I wrote:

My mind travels beyond places that are routine or common. I find myself thinking about traveling spiritually. I am a bit frightened because I have almost accepted the possibility that I may be one of God's creations meant to serve as a cautionary lesson to others. I am no longer sure if I will be the one out of thirty-six people who will survive addiction.

I am tired of my off-and-on habit and the life I live. My life is a series of "new beginnings" (jobs, homes, rules), and quite frankly, I would rather be with Christ. It is almost as if the "spirit of fear" has made a home in my flesh. Most of the time I am neutral, experiencing no intense emotions – not much anger, no real joy or exuberance either. I've become the walking dead.

When I look in the mirror, I see an attractive woman who is a slave. I've allowed my temple to deteriorate. My hands and feet have become gray and old-looking and my eyes have lost the purity of the little girl who wants out! Where I was once an endless source of adrenaline, enthusiasm, and focused goals, I am now a fearful woman. I no longer have the same inner worthiness I once had.

I believe drugs were intentionally created, by those who have no God, to seek and destroy as many as possible – not just the suffering addict, but the lives of parents who must watch their child suffer, lose everything over and over again, struggle to rebuild their lives, and then start another cycle of active addiction. It's a domino effect that knocks out one child at a time. It also takes down one family at a time as they, too, lose hope.

I need to warn all those with a curious nature: Ask God to spare you from this life of highs and lows, of too many losses of friends, careers, lovers and dreams. When the energy of chemicals unfold within your soul, a clash of forces takes place. You will begin to behave in a way that doesn't align with being a child of God. Once the energy dies and you come in touch with your soul again, the guilt will overwhelm you. This is the clashing.

I made Al many promises over the three years we dated. He would want a guarantee that I would never drink again. Each time, I would promise it was the last time. And in those moments, I always meant it.

Toward the end of our third year together, Al promised he would propose by Christmas. We spent the holidays with my parents, and I really thought it was going to happen then. Mom and Dad wanted to renew their vows. My dad re-proposed to my mom. It was a beautiful moment. They were crying; we were crying. It seemed like the perfect opportunity for Al to ask me for my hand in marriage. It was Christmas, and I thought, *Now it's my turn.*

A month later, Al kept his promise, and against my sponsor's advice, I said, "yes."

The year of our engagement was amazing. We had so many beautiful moments with family and friends. We celebrated our love for one another with wedding showers, family gatherings and long weekends at the beach with Mia. It was also challenging. I drank once, but Al stuck with me.
He just said he saw the best in me.

I really tried to be a super stepmom and wife-to-be. I overproduced at work and won all kinds of awards. I truly did my best to be a contribution to the world – despite my quiet concerns about my worthiness and ability to remain sober. I prayed for a renewed mind. I went to recovery meetings and did my step work faithfully. At times I felt invincible. But, at that time, 12 months seemed to be my record for sobriety.

Saying 'I DO'

"For we ourselves were once foolish, disobedient,
led astray, slaves to various passions and
pleasures, passing our days in malice and envy.
But when the goodness and loving kindness of
God our Savior appeared, he saved us."

(TITUS 3)

Chapter Fourteen

A year after our engagement, I walked down the aisle and said, "I do" to Al. It's still an excruciating memory and is difficult to write about it in this book, even today. However, in the spirit of full disclosure, I knew God's unconditional love and faithfulness would be revealed, if I allowed you to see *inside* my most painful memory. This sorrow is far beyond being deaf as a little girl and the ridicule I endured. It is more painful than the kidnapping or the years of intermittent struggles. I prayed for courage to share this story so that you would see that God heals even the deepest wounds and regrets. I never spoke about it to anyone; it's still too raw at this point in my life. Until now, 15 years later.

Even though I met Al at a steakhouse instead of a royal ball, I knew I had found my Prince Charming. Living a sober life was shaping up to be perfect. Looking back, I realize my fatal flaw was not that I didn't invite God into my life, but that I didn't fully surrender. Externally, I appeared to submit to God's will, yet on the inside, I was not surrendering my life to God.

We had every detail perfectly planned. It was important to us that close family and friends played an integral role. The flower arrangements were handmade by special friends; the tender wedding scriptures from the book of Corinthians and Psalms were specially selected to include God's promises for marriage and were read by my godmother and best companions. The reception included family favorite polka songs. The church was beautifully decorated with fresh flowers, candelabras and dim lighting.

The ambiance inside the hotel ballroom was exquisite with gold tapered candles, fine linen tablecloths and tailored chair covers. Instead of table numbers, we labeled each with attributes of a successful marriage: ambition, passion, commitment, and love. I wanted every guest to feel as though they were the bride and groom. The church service was in dim lighting, and I deliberately chose a small cathedral so each guest could hear the exchange of our vows.

As the guests inside awaited the service, the bridal party was lined up, two by two, waiting for the music to begin. I was in the back of the church, anxiously poised to walk up the aisle when I heard the wedding song play. As I stepped out of the bridal room and turned the corner, our eyes met, my father's and mine. His face flushed with surprise at the beauty of his little girl, all grown up and dressed in white lace and shimmering crystal beadwork. Tears welled up in his eyes, and his chest expanded, as though to catch his breath. I gracefully walked towards him, smiling with excitement and pure joy. I tenderly reached out to him with gratitude and felt overwhelmed with adoration for the man who stood by my side. My dad was an integral part of my life in each victory and was a strong spiritual warrior in moments of distress. From this day forward, he would no longer be the sole man in my life. He would hand me over to another whom I would love deeply. He, too, was overcome with emotion. We both gained our composure and walked down the aisle, elated this day had finally come.

The service was everything Al and I planned. The church procession was perfect. Mia, Al, and I took our vows as a family. The wedding reception was high-energy and love-filled. We were introduced to our guests as husband and wife, and I was happier than I had ever been. We danced our first song to Marc Cohn's *True Companion*, and I knew I was safe in Al's arms. The traditional wedding toasts were sincere. It was a sacred space.

Al and I made rounds to the tables and welcomed every guest. I spent most of the night with family, dancing to our favorite tunes.

In a naive act of loyalty, I made the mistake of inviting some of the people from my past to our wedding. I fooled myself into thinking they were friends who deserved to witness my special day, because once I decided to get sober, they supported my decision. There they were, smiling and cheering as I danced around in my white gown. But what happened next reawakened the demon of addiction within me.

After dancing with my husband, I sipped on my ginger ale. Al and I took a seat in front of the room, along with the bridal party. My father got up to toast the celebration, told funny stories from my childhood, and shared his quirky jokes about what it takes to have a successful marriage. His attention turned to Al. "As my new son-in-law, you should know the two words that have saved my marriage — and created harmony between Sandy and I for more than thirty years — will also save you from having arguments with Mary Katherine. When in doubt, Al, simply look at Mary Katherine and say, 'Yes, dear,' and quickly walk away." The 250 guests cheered and laughed aloud.

Suddenly, I was distracted from my dad's speech, when a waiter set two flutes in front of me. The waiter discreetly pointed out that one glass was ginger ale and the other was champagne. My father continued to tell a funny story about me as a child, but I could no longer laugh along with the guests. My attention was no longer on my new husband or my sweet father, but on the two identical glasses in front of me. The only way I can describe it is the room faded away, and those glasses came into sharp focus. Like Alice in *Through the Looking-Glass*, sipping from one would keep me there, sober and jovial, the perfect bride with my perfect husband; the other foretold broken promises and shattered dreams. With almost 12 months of sobriety behind me, I justified the drink by telling myself it was **my** *wedding* and I *deserved* it for all my hard work.

Most of the night was picture-perfect, and I managed to limit myself to only a few drinks. However, my memory gets blurry later in the evening. For that reason, I'll let my friends and family members share their recollections of my wedding.

Karla says:

The party was going fine. It wasn't until the end of the reception when Mary Katherine came into the reception hall and said something bizarre to the girl sitting next to me.

It was so obvious. The beautiful woman had disappeared, and the disease and the spirit of addiction took over.

When I saw Mary Katherine like that, I felt like she would never make it out of addiction alive. If you can't make it through your own wedding reception, I thought...

Al weighs in what he saw:

At the reception, she and I went around to everybody's tables laughing, celebrating and having a wonderful time as husband and wife. Then, towards the end of the evening as guests were leaving, I just noticed she went from good to bad, and downhill fast. I asked her, "Have you been drinking?"

I remember being inside the honeymoon suite crying, because I couldn't figure out what went wrong. I had only had one glass of champagne and a few drinks. I went into the bathroom and found my dress in a heap on the floor. *How can this be happening to me?* I asked myself. No matter how much I tried to snap out of it and regain my composure, the "mind rush" would not stop and the room spun out of control. If I lay very still, I could remain calm. It was another moment I wished I was dead. I prayed that God would take me home to heaven. By taking that first glass of champagne, had I set this nightmare in motion? Was this my punishment for choosing drink over sobriety?

CHASING
HAPPILY EVER AFTER,
Becoming
FREE

"*Stand confidently in all of your imperfections, beauty and authenticity. You are a child of God.*"

—MARY KATHERINE MORALES

Chapter Fifteen

Marriage was supposed to be my happily-ever-after, the fairytale ending to this cautionary tale. But, like a lit match tossed into gasoline, the spark that was lit at the wedding gave way to the inferno of my addiction. It raged and consumed every waking and sleeping thought.

My soul was once again consumed with fear. I would try to pull myself together, attending meetings, church groups and treatment programs, only to fall back into the depths of addiction. It was one step forward and two steps back, and I was growing spiritually and physically weaker. Through it all, Al and I remained committed to each other. Our love for one another was solid, and we believed that if we prayed together and continued to trust in God, I could rise to the call upon my life. His unconditional love was my saving grace.

My last experience with active addition came a few days after I had signed up for an outpatient treatment program. I had been in outpatient care for three days when I succumbed to the raging addiction living inside my body and mind. I was consumed with anxiety, and my nervous system felt like it was hotwired to an electrical circuit. Even asleep, I wasn't at peace. My life belonged to a power greater than me, an evil power. The Devil had me by the throat and was trying to kill me.

That final spree lasted ten days. I packed my suitcase and ran to my usual high-end hotel, overwhelmed. I was in touch with Al every couple of hours. Daily, he would remind me, "Mary Katherine, you are loved by so many. Don't give up. There is a way out."

On Easter Sunday, he answered the phone, and his voice wasn't much louder than a whisper. I didn't bother to hide my concern. I told him it felt like I was dying on this Holy Day, that I was slowly fading into the void. Too desperate to fight, we both cried and promised to hold on for one more day. I felt so alone. Talking to Al was too painful. After hanging up, I wept.

The battle I fought off and on for years had come to a crossroads — live or die.

"Mary Katherine didn't know it, but Al and I started talking two or three times a day," my mom says. "I admire him. He's a good man, a good father, a good husband, a good son-in-law. I only wished for them to hang on."

Al explains:

As her new husband and soulmate, I was crushed with fear that my new, beautiful wife was so sick. I would pray for hours, hoping she would make it one more day. I pleaded with God not to take her from me and her family. I shouted to God, "You know how hard she is fighting, so bring her home to me!" I would wait each day for the call and the small voice on the other end.

Though I was extremely disappointed in Mary Katherine, I also knew she was in the fight of her life. Mary Katherine loved me; that I knew. I didn't want to give up on her because deep inside, I understood her battle was intensely bigger than what she could do alone. As her life-mate, I had to fight against the malevolent force with her, not against her.

I no longer felt as if I was fighting internal demons; I began to see them as well. Some people would say I was hallucinating, that I was having a psychotic break due to lack of sleep and food, but I truly believe that good and evil spirits exist in the spiritual realm. These were entities who are separated from God; they walk the spiritual streets of the abyss. The only difference between us was that these spirits had actually crossed over into the afterlife, and I was still physically alive. They had been deceived.

I saw a tall, thin young man dressed in black clothes, leaning against a truck. He had a smirk on his face as he stared in my direction. His arms were folded, and he appeared to be waiting for me to become more vulnerable, mentally and spiritually. He wanted me to lose my mind as the night grew darker. I knew he was doomed and had nowhere to go, as there is no reference to time in Hell, so he stood there patiently and watched my every move. Job 4:14-17 says, "Fear came upon me, and trembling, which made all my bones shake. Then a spirit passed before my face; the hair on my body stood up. It stood still, but I could not discern its appearance. A form *was* before my eyes. There was silence, then a voice *saying*, "Can a mortal be more righteous than God? Can a man be more pure than his Maker?'"

At 4:00 a.m., I finally spoke to the entity out loud. "I am still a child of God, even though I struggle," I shouted. "You cannot take me to the dark side. I will not give up my faith in Christ, even now. The Lord will rescue me from my darkness and my addiction, and I will be redeemed. I can still overcome my addiction."

Exhausted, I knew it was time to go home. I had a moment of clarity. Thank God. My spiritual battle aligned with the person described in the book of Matthew 12: 43-45, "When an unclean spirit goes out of a man, he goes through dry places, seeking rest and finds none. Then he says, 'I will return to my house from which I came.' And when he comes, he finds it empty, swept, and put in order. Then he goes and takes with him seven other spirits more wicked than himself, and they enter and dwell there; and the last state of that man is worse than the first. So, shall it be with this wicked generation."

I prayed for help, reciting a memorized prayer over and over as a mantra, "I can do all things through Christ who strengthens me." I prayed that this would be the day I would experience freedom – for a lifetime.

My substance use disorder, the clashing story of unworthiness and the horrible experience of shame ended where the first chapter of this book began, exhausted in that messy hotel room. After a night of seeing spirits and praying for sobriety, my life changed. I surrendered. I found the courage to call Al and told him I was ready to accept help.

Through a moment of divine grace and clarity, I chose life over death.

Climbing in his truck, Al delivered a plan: "You are going to treatment so you can get the medical attention you deserve." I didn't have the energy to refuse his conditions. Defeated and exhausted, I submitted to Al's plan. Though my body throbbed with pain from the abuse, my heart stopped hurting. I knew my journey through Hell was over.

Though I accepted Al's ultimatum without resistance, I became really upset with "this Susan woman" from the treatment center. She told me I needed to come in immediately. "Just give me a day to sleep, and I will consider it," I bargained, suddenly concerned Al would leave me upon my entrance to treatment. My emotions and mind were totally maxed out, and I became irrational. I screamed – literally – into the phone and demanded rest and food. Al told me he would take me to another hotel. We checked in, and I showered. Of course, Al refused to leave. He watched me sleep for 13 hours straight.

He got me up and dressed me for treatment. I begged for more sleep, but he wasn't having it. He knew that I needed medical attention. The offer was the same. I could go to treatment or go back to the chaos I knew too well.

The pain I felt getting out of the shower the day before was only the beginning of the tenderness I felt as my feet hit the ground after sleeping all those hours. My legs and feet were so sore, I could hardly walk. Brushing my hair actually hurt. My gums were tender as the toothbrush swept across each tooth. I was less than 110 pounds.

I could hardly stand in the shower, because my legs were so weak, and my feet and ankles hurt. My hip bones protruded from lack of food, and my chin and face were sore to the touch. My teeth and ears hurt. Overwhelmed with fatigue, I stepped out of the water, dried off and took a look at myself in the large mirror. All I saw was a tattered woman with tired eyes, drawn cheeks and sores on my chin. My body was just about dead. That my heart didn't give out is a true miracle. I had given my body every reason to stop functioning properly, and I had done my nervous system serious harm with the substances, alcohol and lack of sleep. My soul was depleted, and my spirit-man was vulnerable and weak.

Yet, I was filled with gratitude that my love affair with God – through it all – was still intact.

I am forever thankful for Al. The commitment he had made before God and the church kept him in the marriage. I could only imagine when he agreed to stay with me "for better or for worse" that he never imagined how heartbreaking "worse" could be.

In the mirror, I asked myself, "Do I go into treatment, or take my chances and go it on my own?" My mind raced in and out of my options. One moment, I considered the promise of getting better and restoring peace to my life. The next moment, I was frantic with thoughts of *"What have I done?" "How did I get here?"* and *"What does my future have in store?"* I could hardly breathe as I weighed my choices.

I was full of both gratitude and anger when I decided Watershed Treatment Center was my destination. I would live in a hospital setting, not for a couple days, but for what might be months. I had been down this long, winding road, where therapists demand details and truth, freedom disappears, men withdraw, family members recoil, and employers fire people – like me.

The love and support from my family and friends held me up during my time in treatment and throughout my early recovery. Now, more than 15 years later, it is my turn to support others – from all walks of life and with all kinds of challenges — and remind them that God is a God of transformations.

But it was a conversation I had two weeks after checking in that changed my life forever. "Sit down in that chair," Dr. Getty said. I took a seat in the cafeteria. "Mary Katherine, I'm going to share something with you, and you have to listen. I've been doing this for twenty years. Never in my life have I met someone who is as heartbroken as your husband, Al. I'm here to tell you that Al is not a man that is going to watch you go in and out of treatment for a lifetime. He's going to have to say goodbye to you, because he is physically incapable of watching you check in and out of hospitals. He's completely heartbroken, and he's wondering what the hell he's gotten himself into being married to you. But he loves you more than life, and if you want recovery, his commitment to you and your marriage is solid.

"Your life is like a crystal ball. Inside that ball, there's a person who has had a more amazing life than anyone I've ever met in my work. Although you have experienced a great deal of trauma, you have shared some incredible life moments and great success in your life. You've entertained movie stars and celebrities, you've had an astonishing career, and when you're sober, people absolutely adore you. You have the power to impact people in a significant way. But the crystal ball is completely cracked with hairline fractures, and if you ever relapse again, it'll be the ping that shatters it completely.

"Your life will never look or sound the same again. You will lose Al, Mia, your family, your career, your freedom and possibly your life. I need you to go back to your room, get on your knees, and ask yourself what life means to you. Ask God for direction. Do you want Al in your life? Do you want your job? Do you want Mia as a daughter? Do you want to live your life coming in and out of hospitals and treatment centers? If anyone of these areas is important to you, you must know the truth about what I see."

My heart plunged into my stomach as I went back to my room.

I got on my knees, and it was there, for the first time, I knew I had what it takes to get clean. I felt the gentle nudging of the Holy Spirit, also known as The Spirit of Truth, and a refreshed sense of hope.

Kneeling alongside my bed, I intently prayed for a new life. The remorse and reality of what I had done and who I had become set in. I sat for a long time in that silent room with Dr. Getty's words echoing through my mind.

After intense soul-searching, I fell into a deep self-reflection as I agonized about the consequences of my actions towards Al. Motivated by this concern, I completed all the assigned work and asked for additional ways I could create a meaningful life. I finally faced my personal Four Horsemen: Terror, Bewilderment, Frustration and Despair. Facing each horseman head-on, I became willing to reveal the intense pain I still carried from my past. I admitted that, like a prisoner sentenced to life behind bars, I too had given up my dreams long ago. I cried healing tears on many days.

As I cried, I remembered a line from *Dicken's Great Expectations:* "Heaven knows we need never be ashamed of our tears, for they are rain upon the blinding dust of earth, overlying our hard hearts." My grief was satisfied and carried away by my tears. I stood before judge and jury, willing to own up to my mistakes and accept the consequences.

I was ready to Become a Woman of Principle and live a courageous life.

My counselors were amazed by my zeal. Any free moment I had between attending 12-Step meetings and completing assignments, I spent in prayer and reflection. I went to grad school, got a two-year certificate in theological studies, became a competitive long-distance cyclist and rebuilt all my relationships based on principles like transparency. I knew that my work towards rebuilding my character was a daily practice and felt my relationship with Christ was reborn. I never thought I'd feel optimistic again, but every day I stayed sober, this little mustard seed of hope grew and flourished in my soul.

I became an honest woman with an impeccable reputation.

But this growth was not my work alone. Besides the counselors, Al dedicated hours to attending joint therapy sessions and loving me back to soundness of mind. He was my biggest fan, as I became the woman God had always intended

What is amazing is that Al also began to rise to the call upon his own life and experience the kind of freedom and joy he had never known. He was becoming the man he had always dreamed of being.

Over the past 15 years, the journey towards a healthy, trusting relationship has been a transformative experience. We have a fantastic marriage based on the truths of God, intimacy and trust. He is my best friend and soulmate. Because we have practiced becoming wise through putting God first, everything else in our marriage is automatically set in divine order. Today, we have more joy than words can express.

I believe my marriage broke the curse I had been living under during my substance use disorder. Scripture talks about how the braid of three is harder to sever than a strand of one or two. Ecclesiastes 4:12 states, "A person standing alone can be attacked and defeated, but two can stand back-to-back and conquer." Three are even better, for a triple-braided cord is not easily broken." When Al and I took our vows, the darkness in me no longer had just me to deal with. It was Al, me and The Holy Spirit. It was that vow we took before Christ and the deep bond it forged that saved me. When I walked out of treatment, I was released from the bondage of the lies of unworthiness, of my demons, of my addiction. The Four Dark Horsemen, who once influenced my mindset and determined my behavior, stood behind Four Devout Warriors: *Honesty, Integrity, Gratitude, and Hope.* Through the Spirit of Truth, I became a Woman of Principle, and I had a relationship with God.

I
WAS
FINALLY
FREE.

Transforming **YOUR**

MIND

...AND LIVING

COURAGEOUSLY

M.K. 2.0:

WHAT IS A
WOMAN
—— OF ——
PRINCIPLE

"But, we all, with unveiled face, beholding as in a mirror the glory of the Lord, are being transformed into the same image from glory to glory, just as by the Spirit of the Lord."

(2 CORINTHIANS 3:18)

Dear Women of Principle, Know that you can:

- *Live a transforming life and step into the rising of your call.*

- *Stand boldly in the face of challenges and make excellent choices.*

- *Reflect the characteristics of God and walk in the fullness of the Holy Spirit.*

- *Impact the people you love by daring to become the 2.0 version of YOU.*

As I forewarned in the Introduction, you were invited through the first section of this book to travel with me on the *journey through hell to home*. It was a transformative journey where my story of unworthiness clashed with the bold promises of God, and it was the beginning of my *Becoming a Woman of Principle*.

Having read my story, you understand why many who see me today want to know how I untangled myself from such a complex and tight-knit web of poor decisions, consequences, and spiritual and emotional turmoil. The truth is nothing about it was easy. But I was faced with the choice to either stay the woman I had become during that decade of torture or figure out a way, with God's help and the support of His angels on earth, to slowly and intentionally untangle the mess of my life, one strand at a time.

I realize I am not the only woman who has suffered the consequences of poor choices, dangerous circumstances and the gift of desperation to find the blessings of peace and significance. I know amazing women from all walks of life who have overcome insurmountable challenges: the loss of a child, crippling illnesses, a variety of addictions, a devasting loss of home or finances, divorce, losing a self-defining career, major depression or mental health disorders. I pray that my transparency and courage to become a Woman of Principle and the 2.0 version of myself will be an inspiration for you to discover your own 2.0 life. Your 2.0 life is the empowered version where you are transformed in your mind, living courageously and rising to the call upon your life.

You may be faced with a choice today also. Some days, that choice won't be easy — it certainly wasn't for me. But I stand as a living witness that the conscious commitment to five practices will help realign, reinvent and transform you into the Woman of Principle you have always desired to be.

What exactly is a Woman of Principle?

Simply put, a Woman of Principle stands on the fundamental truths of scripture that states she is valued, chosen, adopted, accepted, predestined and marvelously and wonderfully made. Our lives reflect the belief that we can be who God says we can be, and we can have the life God intended.

Praise God, I conceded to my inner-most self that I was a woman suffering from Substance use disorder — a mind, body and spiritual disease. I finally opened my heart to receive the awesome blessings of grace, as a beloved and accepted child of God. As they were for me, these blessings are available to us all – every day.

My journey of Becoming a Woman of Principle has given me spiritual authority over evil, according to the power that works in me through the Holy Spirit. Now I understand that in every phase of my life there's a love affair between me and God. Like a knight in shining armor, The Holy Spirit provided protection and care – even when the odds stacked against me. When the world said, "She won't make it; she's too far gone," the promise of God said otherwise. I was on my knees *somewhere* passionately praying for the strength to live one more day. With hope, I looked to God, praying for the courage to make good choices. I begged God to silence the hateful comments in my mind, which said, "You do not have what it takes to get sober! You are no longer an amazing, All-American woman; your dreams are no longer possible. It is time to give up!" And, despite the overwhelming physical cravings, I intuitively knew that I was a child of God, loved eternally and I would rise out of the miry clay. It is time for you to rise as well. You are surrounded by the arms of God and the songs of deliverance and love. No matter your challenge, you are a courageous, transforming Woman of Principle.

As a Woman of Principle, you are developing the characteristics of God. Before you think, "That is impossible," remember the book of Ephesians tells us that as we accept the *disciplines* of unity, purity and forgiveness and walk in the fullness of the Holy Spirit, we will have access to true spiritual power. This comes from *practicing* obedience. As we come to understand that our behavior is the most effective sermon we will ever preach, our willingness to diligently practice love and work to model the life of Jesus Christ becomes our focus.

For us to walk a **principled life**, we must first define our values and develop the practices that will define our character. These values and practices will guide you toward unshakable principles that will be your North Star. They will serve as a code of ethics that define for you a new, bold way of being, a deep commitment to Christlike characteristics. As Women of Principle, we will have more authenticity, God-fidence, power, soundness of mind and inner peace. This, in turn, positively impacts our relationships and gives us the courage to face challenges with grace and humility. Our transformed way of being is illuminated by acts of kindness as we shift from a self-focus towards a deep concern for all mankind.

When we recognize that we have been saved by grace, we judge less and love more. Shame steps into the light of God, and unworthiness bows to a bold identity through the Holy Spirit.

My transformation has made all the pain worthwhile. Now, I am liberated to share my circumstances openly because I am free. I know millions of women are experiencing all kinds of everyday challenges and trials that keep them from living up to their fullest potential. I would rather have people *judge my past* than see ONE more woman hide behind closed doors and live under the lies of the enemy and persecution of this superficial world. The shame that once convinced me to hide is replaced with the commitment to live courageously, so all women will step out of the darkness, releasing the B.S. stories and negative agreements that reinforce playing small. It is time to step into the bold call upon your life and walk in light, love and wisdom (Ephesians 5). What are your dreams, Woman of Principle?

The upcoming chapters will teach the practices that led me to live my divine purpose, and they will be a guidepost for you too, no matter what you face. Whether you are a rock star CEO, a powerful force in your community, a devoted stay-at-home mom, a celebrity or a woman aspiring to rebuild your life – this transformative journey will align with your dreams.

The idea is that we ALL rise and that as Women of Principle, we lock arms in love sharing our gifts, talents and experiences so that no one is left wondering if they can achieve their goals.

I am forever thankful to my loved ones who stuck by my side, and I am committed to living my remaining time on Earth showing my thankfulness. How will I show my gratitude? Through spreading the news that our God is a God of second chances, a God of love, and a God of courageous transformations.

How Do You Become a Woman of Principle?

Where do you begin? How do you create, by God's grace, the 2.0 courageously transforming version of yourself, no matter where you stand today in this journey? You decide right here and right now that this is the first day of the rest of your life as a Woman of Principle. You start with courageous honesty, and you build one practice at a time, so deep within you that the enemy can't dare pluck it out.

Your becomingness is your strength.

In my old life, I was consumed by fear and shame. People can be cruel. I was terrified that if people knew my sinful past, their judgment would be harsh and that I would collapse under the weight of their opinions. Because of that fear, I lived within self-protective walls that hindered my spiritual growth and silenced my truth. Placing their opinions of me over God's miracle in my new life eliminated my ability to stand in supernatural power and grace. For a decade, I preferred looking perfect in the eyes of man rather than going for my dream of *becoming* an author, spiritual teacher, accomplished professional and motivational speaker.

I have received a second chance at life – halleluiah – and I want to be the beacon of hope that attracts other women towards their own journey to God.

The five practices in the following chapters are the roadmap I used to Become a Woman of Principle in every area of my life. I walk freely among my peers with the Holy Spirit, holding my head up high and my back straight. I have journeyed through hell to home.

Today and every day ahead, I stand in assurance that I am a Woman of Principle.

I stand on the fundamental truth that I can be who God says I can be, and I can have the life God intended. I am the embodiment of old things being passed away and becoming new.

As Women of Principle, we are being called to rise to our full potential and live in freedom. By definition, freedom means "liberation from slavery or restraint" or "from the power of another." Let's be clear, there are *systems* and *people* in the world trying to control and negatively influence your thinking. You must develop wisdom in order to decipher the facts, as well as the interpretations that will position you to live your best life. In my old life, I didn't live in freedom. I lived under false teachings and half-truths that led me down the path of self-destructive behaviors. Dear sisters, can you relate? Have you ever made decisions based on half-truths or superficiality, which led you towards regret? Have you ever chosen to *be right* or *look good* in a conversation, instead of being kind or being honest? We have all operated under the false teachings of this world, and we have all been impacted by them.

The world is full of books, media platforms and personalities, podcasters and educators, who are well-intentioned but do not know the truths of God. That is okay. I am not blaming them or standing in a place of judgment. However, as a Woman of Principle, you can help guide the world towards the love of God and allow His supernatural wisdom to transform your mind and light your path. Others will follow.

There are also those in leadership and "spiritual teachers" who intentionally draw people from God and the divine wisdom of scripture because they have an agenda to control your mind. Make no mistake, their goals are to create communities where people forget how to think for themselves. They proclaim peace and independence, but they are purposely creating systems to control, manipulate and divide us.

Being a Woman of Principle means understanding *some* of the fundamental truths of scripture and knowing how to activate those truths so we can choose thriving over surviving. At one point in my journey, I wanted spirituality, success and sobriety handed to me on a silver platter, instead of taking a disciplined and mature approach to life. I did not know anything about the Bible, and I had limited knowledge about recovery and powerful distinctions in servant leadership. I learned the hard way that we cannot deliver ourselves from sin or mistaken identity, and we cannot have an *anointed* freedom, unless we know God personally and intimately.

According to Jack W. Hayford, biblical wisdom unites God, the Source of all understanding, with daily life, where principles of right living are put into practice.

(Hayford, J. (2004). *The Hayford Bible Handbook:* Thomas Nelson).

Throughout scripture, God tells us to ask for wisdom, for it will lead to powerful insights and practical applications in your family, friendships, career and community.

As illustrated in the earlier chapters, I tried every way possible to *fix* myself, whether it was a better job, a better relationship, more friends, more social events, a better wardrobe, a better apartment, etc. But these were merely temporary solutions, never substantial or long-lasting. I still had that nagging hole in my heart. I was a slave to quick fixes. What are you a slave to today? Remember, dear sisters, there is no condemnation in the journey of transformation. Common addictions like looking good, being right at all costs, lack of discipline over finances, deprived health habits and poor communication in our families and businesses are killing intimate relationships and our dreams of abundant living. Offenses such as pornography, theft, drugs, white-collar crimes and driving under the influence are stealing our good standing in the communities in which we serve. We are caving to thought processes and behaviors that keep us stuck, because we lack the humility and the supernatural power of God in our lives. But the time is now. We are, in fact, being called to release old thought patterns and behaviors and RISE, in order to live courageously while making a positive impact in the world.

If you've learned anything from my story, I hope it is that the way to freedom is transformation through a renewal of our minds and a relationship with the Holy Spirit.

When I was 14 and the Spirit of God literally gave me the direction that I would write a book, I had absolutely no idea it would be a book based on my poor choices and failures. I heard the call a second time in my thirties while suffering as an addict. I was shouting to God for help, and the Holy Spirit almost audibly stated, *You will recover, and you will write a book about your journey through hell to home. Yeah, right!* was my response. Clearly, the Holy Spirit didn't know how vain I was or how terrified I was of 'your' opinion of me and my imperfections. I swore I would never tell anyone about the degree to which I failed – repeatedly.

I would have never believed, as a little girl and young woman, I would encounter so much pain and turmoil, yet happily live to tell about it. Not only did God command me to share my story of victory in a small room with those who can relate to my trials, but to the world. So, let me be clear about my intentions. It isn't to over-qualify, be inappropriately vulnerable, elicit pity or talk about me ad nauseam. Rather, the purpose is to provide the kind of power that lies in storytelling and transparency so that other women relate, apply and rise to their calling. The world is desperate for women who are deeply connected to the source of love, whose perspectives are rooted in experience, relatability and humility. It's the only way transformation works.

Since the inception of this book, God has taken it a step further, because He is all-knowing, and revealed to me five lifechanging practices that refine our character and allow us to stand in supernatural principles that become our North Star for living. These are the five practices that allowed me to *Become* a Woman of Principle. They are hard-won, sincere and lifechanging. I propose they are the foundational distinctions that will provide you with access to divine revelations, which will refine your character. You can apply them to your everyday living, at all phases of your *transforming* and *rising* journey. They will give you the courage to live the life you have always dreamed of.

I Know These Five Practices
Will Do The Same For You:

PRACTICE **1.** Becoming Beautifully Transparent through the Practice of **SIMPLE HONESTY**

PRACTICE **2.** Becoming Impeccable through the Practice of **BEING YOUR WORD**

PRACTICE **3.** Becoming Generous through the Practice of **SERVANT LEADERSHIP**

PRACTICE **4.** Becoming Victorious through the Practice of **RUNNING WITH CHAMPIONS**

PRACTICE **5.** Becoming Wise through the Practice of **GOD FIRST**

Defining Values, Practices and Principles

Let's take a moment before exploring the five life-changing practices to help you understand the differences between the three terms in context of what is being relayed in *Becoming Woman of Principle*.

What is a Value?

According to the *Merriam-Webster Dictionary*, values are qualities intrinsically valuable or desirable.

In Dr. Brené Brown's book, *Dare to Lead*, she adds, "A value is a way of being or believing that we hold most important." It also states that we must be able to name our values in order to live them. Values are beliefs and opinions that people hold regarding specific ideas or issues and are ultimately subjective, internal and flexible. They may change as demands or needs change. If a belief or opinion is something that may change depending upon the conditions, then it is a value.

We have seen where companies outwardly display their Values next to the Mission and Vision, so employees are familiar and can use these as a guide for how they work. What are the core values that guide your thoughts, decisions and actions today and how can they be tweaked in your state of transformation to a Woman of Principle?

What is a Practice?

A practice is an activity you repeat to improve a skill. What we practice, we become. Practices develop habits. Within each practice, there is an underlying value. Our goal is to "activate" the skill within each practice in order to *become* what we practice. The *becoming* process is connecting the skill to the impact on our lives and humanity.

In the pages that follow, you will be given ways you can apply the five practices in your daily living. These repeatable actions will help in *Becoming* a Woman of Principle.

What is a Principle?

After values are established and practices or habits are formed, there is a fundamental truth upon which systems of beliefs and morals are formed. These are called principles. Principles are timeless and help us to determine our values when we face challenging circumstances.

*The important distinction between a value and
a principle is that a principle is a guide for a
behavior, not a belief.*

So, it becomes less about what you believe and more about how you act and show up in the world when it comes to principles.

Principles are understood as a code of ethics that transcend time and circumstance. As we take time to establish a set of principles, we create a compass that we can refer to anytime we are in doubt or when you need to take a stand or evaluate any particular behavior, situation or opportunity. Remember, they are the fundamental "base you stand upon when you make everyday choices."

Your principles are what you *become* after values are established and new habits that align with these values are formed. As you begin to incorporate the following five Practices into your daily living, may God bless and keep you on your journey to *Becoming a Woman of Principle.*

NOW, LET'S GET *started!*

1.

Becoming
BEAUTIFULLY
TRANSPARENT
— THROUGH —
SIMPLE
HONESTY

"So, Jesus said to the Jews who had believed him, "If you abide in my word, you are truly my disciples, and you will know the truth, and the truth will set you free."

(JOHN 8: 31-32))

Dear Women of Principle, Know that you can:

- *Choose simple honesty in tough conversations and embrace the challenges that come with being an honest woman.*

- *Invent a new future through the practice of honesty.*

- *Stand outside of yourself, observe your thinking and choose to be honest in all your affairs.*

- *Avoid the physiological, emotional and spiritual consequences of lying.*

My beautiful soul sisters, it takes courage to be honest. And, it takes a real commitment to be radically honest. Being honest — at every level — isn't for the feeble or the faint at heart. It is for the awakening woman. This practice is for the brave individual, willing to take an honorable stand for humanity. This transformative way of living means we humbly face the reasons why we are tempted to tell white lies; we pause, face the fears and choose honesty. *Sigh.*

As we come to understand what dishonesty is and how it damages us and those we love, we will find honesty as a **bold stand for love.** This chapter is designed to help you *Become* a Woman of Principle, a woman who is simply honest and wholeheartedly authentic, with the ability to stand outside of yourself, observe your thinking and choose to be honest in all your affairs.

I lovingly challenge you today to become unwavering in this practice called *Honesty*. At the most basic level, practicing the foundational principle of simple honesty means sticking to the facts, not embellishing in our language during interactions and making honesty a way of being. For those of us who have mastered the basics, becoming beautifully transparent through this practice is about mastering the nuances of emotional intelligence and radical honesty.

Simple Honesty is a Way of Being

To live honestly is a way of being. It is a deep commitment to self-awareness and requires the commitment to answering hard questions about our worldview, our character and our moral behaviors. It is also the path to freedom and joy. Many scientists who study the mind and human behavior would tell you, to lie is to be human. I get it. Telling the truth can be challenging. There is no shortage of scientific articles that explain *why* people lie. At the root of it – the answer is simple. We want to protect ourselves or a person, place or thing we have deemed as more important than telling the truth. Be warned, though. This is a slippery slope. The very person or thing we believe to be more important than being honest is at risk when we tell the white lie to protect it.

Early on in my journey, when I made the commitment to walk in love and sobriety, I realized that becoming an honest woman was the lifeline for my sobriety and, ultimately, my life. Over time, I learned my language and my ways of being had become riddled with white lies, and I had compromised my integrity to look good, play it safe and be right. I lied to hide my battle with addiction. Even when I got sober, my perfectionism, which is a whole other chapter in my life, made being honest challenging. Because the root of perfectionism is shame and unworthiness, it tempts you to embellish the truth to cover shame and unworthiness. Anyone relate? In order to become a Woman of Principle, I was committed to master my inner world by choosing to transform my mind, use my free will to love others and make excellent choices.

The God First practice, which incorporates prayer and meditation, was critical for becoming an honest woman. I came to understand our divine nature is to live in the light of God. One cannot walk in the light of God and deliberately tell lies – white lies or obvious lies. Slowly, through making conscious contact with God and incorporating practices into our lives, we can develop the skills and the courage to *be* honest – in all our affairs.

According to an article written in *Greater Good Magazine*, titled, "How to Grow the Good in Your Brain," "There is a saying in neuroscience: **Neurons that fire together, wire together.** All mental activity is based on underlying neural activity. Intense, prolonged, or repeated mental/neural activity—especially if it is conscious—will leave an enduring imprint in neural structure, like a surging current reshaping a riverbed. Mental states become neural traits. Day after day, your mind is building your brain." According to science, we were not designed to tell lies, gossip or harm people with our words. This is also supported by scripture. God himself said, "I gave you the spirit of love, power and a sound mind." The good news is that we can change our choices as we change our minds.

We have all spoken words that diminish the light in others. We have all used our power to harm others – sometimes intentionally and sometimes unintentionally. Quite frankly, if you have gossiped, created division, smeared someone's reputation or intentionally called up your BFF during a heated moment and exaggerated the truth to get her to "back you up," then you, my dear sister, have in fact been deceitful.

It's okay. I am certainly not condemning your past. I have one too. I am committed to your victory. I see you living your very best life – every day.

We must humbly acknowledge our strengths, weaknesses and areas where we can expand our knowledge in order to live as Women of Principle.

The principle of honesty is the most powerful tool in our spiritual arsenal to become a powerful vessel for the Holy Spirit to reach the brokenhearted and bring joy to other women.

The practice of honesty promotes intimacy and connection. Honesty opens the door to the truth.

Once, I was in a meeting and a man named Joe made a powerful statement, "There are many levels of honesty, but there is only one truth." Having the courage to be honest is like climbing the stairs. With each step we take to be honest, we are one step closer to experiencing the supernatural truths and the promises of God.

Jesus told us that those who abide in His word will know the truth and the truth will set you free. And not being honest will do just the opposite.

Dishonesty Causes Brain Damage

Embellishing, omitting facts and stretching the truth have become a part of our culture. It's no longer a conscious thing. It's just how we operate and get through this thing called life.

The culture of lies and deception surrounds us. It is an epidemic. Look around you. Many of our political, religious and world leaders are dishonest with their constituents to advance their own priorities. It has become an accepted form of getting what you want, despite the obvious consequences inflicted on other people. Our political leaders justify their lies, because they want to win an election or persuade communities to vote in a particular direction. Most of us justify ours by saying things like, "I had to lie, or I would have lost my job, hurt someone's feelings, or...". When we tell white lies, they lead to manipulation, which is a form of lying. We want what we want, and we are willing to jeopardize our very souls (mind, will and intellect) to get it. The book of Luke reminds us, "For nothing is hidden that will not be made manifest, nor is anything secret that will not be known and come to light." According to well-known author Dr. Stephen Covey, "Every exaggeration of the truth once detected by others destroys our credibility and makes all that we do and say suspect."

Over the 21 years I have been in recovery, I have experienced both of these statements to be true. I have met thousands of people in the program. What I have learned is a person's inability or unwillingness to get honest prevents them from getting well. They spend their days hiding behind a false sense of pride, while their addiction is doing push-ups in the parking lot. Many die with a broken heart, not only from the disease of substance abuse but from the disease of being dishonest. This disease of dishonesty creates the illusion of being "separate from" the world, which creates more shame and fear. It is a vicious cycle. I firmly believe dishonesty is one of the root causes of addiction and brain health disorders.

In the program, we also have individuals who are free from the drinking problem but never truly experience peace and freedom, because they have adopted a habit we call half-truths. Their language is riddled with white lies. These white lies limit their God-given power and prevent them from rising to their full potential. People who consistently tell white lies experience more anxiety, concern and disconnection. This phenomenon is also true for individuals outside the program of recovery. Half-truths are disguised with good intentions, but their long-term consequences are dire.

Dr. Caroline Leaf is one of my favorite scientists and women of faith. In her book, *Switch on Your Brain*, she explains that with each lie, we damage our mind and our physical brain. She explains in great detail that the habit of telling lies also creates brain damage in other people. Lying makes it more difficult to make healthy choices because it is linked to faulty thinking. I can attest that her science has proven to be true in my own journey. When I lied to my family and friends during my addiction, it created turmoil, confusion and grief. They became burdened with my lies. They were affected spiritually, mentally and emotionally by my choices to be dishonest. Addiction is known as a family disease for a reason. When I got well, those closest to me also had wounds that required transformative healing that comes through simple honesty and connection with God.

Think about your own life. Have you ever experienced a disconnection from self and others because of your unwillingness to simply be honest? If so, which area of your life do you have a tendency to tell white lies?

Women of Principle, every lie has a consequence.

This spiritual principle is absolutely neutral to your opinion of it. The transforming power of truth is a universal law that can never be broken, altered or compromised. Like gravity, truth is.

God's thoughts are not your thoughts, or my thoughts, for that matter. He is all-knowing and immutable. He always operates in truths.

When we discipline ourselves to speak in simple truths, we can live in freedom.

As we get into what it means to be a Woman of Principle, honesty is the most profound practice in our code of ethics. Honesty **defines the very nature of our being.** According to Jesus, the heart really matters: "For out of the overflow of the heart the mouth speaks." (Matthew 12:34).

Simple Honesty is the Highest Form of Respect

Respect is directly tied to the practice of honesty. One's commitment to practice honesty demonstrates our willingness to move away from superficial communications and open the door to soulful connections.

Although we are designed for intimacy and love, being honest can be challenging even on our best days. Until we deal with the root causes of why we are tempted to tell white lies, we cannot change. According to an article by John F. Ahearne in the *American Scientist*, "Few would contest the desirability of honesty, and good intentions are nearly universal." As Tina Gunsalus, Director of the National Center for Professional and Research Ethics, observes, "Almost everybody wakes up every day and wants to do the right thing." And yet, by the end of the day, many yield to dishonesty. There are many reasons why white lies trump good thinking and healthy choices.

However, there is hope. The secret is practice, practice, practice. As we transform into a beautifully honest woman, our very nature attracts people towards us. As we make the commitment to be transparent, the truth of God begins to permeate our minds. The supernatural wisdom of God transforms our very being. Why? We are designed for truth. Scripture tells us, in the beginning was the *Word*, and the *Word was God*. What we say matters. Words create the world we live in. The moment we make the decision to use our language for good and we speak honestly – He is faithful to change our hearts towards everything – I mean, everything.

Like a caterpillar who transforms into a beautiful butterfly free to explore flowers in a garden, we too will walk freely in the world.

Over time, my fears disappeared because honesty creates boldness, confidence and peace. As I became honest, clearing the wreckage of my past, I became a woman radiating God-fidence that attracted people towards me. Energetically, I became the vessel for others to feel safe. I became the space and context for women to bring their highest gifts and talents, concerns, shortcomings, victories and life experiences, because they knew that I respected them enough to be honest and loving.

Honesty is about revealing the beauty of your true self. It is about respect and generosity.

It is about being authentic and organic. Honesty is about no more masks. No more fakeness. No more artificial interests. No more interactions with people based on make-believe. When you lie, everything you share with someone isn't real. It's like a movie, right? A movie isn't real – it is a created plot with actors playing out a specific role to influence thoughts and emotions of the audience. When lies exist between two people, essentially each person is playing a character in a movie scene. The villain is treating others with disrespect by playing the role of a sincere person. In contrast, while behind the scenes, the villain has an entirely different motive.

Let me share an extreme example to prove a point.

Adultery is a perfect example of playing the villain. It is an example of someone that begins their journey with a series of what may be defined as harmless white lies. Let me play out the scene for you.

You are a faithful wife with three incredibly talented and beautiful children. You are a stay-at-home mom and you love your life. You see your husband and kids off each day with a kiss, a smile and a prayer. In your heart, you know that being the CEO of your family enterprise is a big job, and you take pride in the organization of the family business. Your kids are well-balanced and engaged in school activities. Your relationship with your husband appears to be solid. In fact, your husband calls each day right before lunch to tell you he loves you, which always brightens your day. From your perspective, your married life seems very good.

One afternoon, just for fun, you decide to have lunch with the girls at a swanky restaurant. You are feeling confident and joyful. As you greet your circle of friends in the bar area, your eye catches a beautiful woman walking by in a glamorous red dress. You cannot help but notice her. She appears warm, sophisticated, and you admire her style. Your eyes meet, and you exchange a heartfelt smile. The moment passes without any further thought. Minutes later, as the maître d escorts you to your table, something else catches your attention. That beautiful blonde whom you admired is sitting next to your husband. The two are intimately leaning into one another and embrace in a kiss. Suddenly, your inner world rages with anger and disbelief. Your heart sinks into your stomach and your pulse races. You ask yourself, "What is happening?" Without pausing, you and your girlfriends in tow, approach the table where your husband looks up from his gaze. His eyes widen as he gasps for air. The once beautiful blonde whom you esteemed now looks scandalous, and she too is shocked by the look on his face. The plot thickens. Out loud, you exclaim, "What is happening?!?" As he begins to provide meaningless excuses, you intuitively know your life has been a lie. The man you trusted for 20 years is now a stranger.

This story can go in any direction from here, ladies. The point is when people lie, relationships end, hearts are broken and dreams are shattered. It can feel like a movie scene as your emotional heart and mind try to untangle the web of deception. The person responsible has methodically placed his cast members into position for his own gains, without any regard. This may be a metaphor, but it's also truth. The truth is when someone gets into the habit of telling white lies, they become BIG lies. Lies are like an avalanche. Momentum builds, and before you know it, it overflows and seeps onto everything and each person within the vicinity, and life as we know it is forever changed. Most of us have been on the receiving end of a lie, so you know it leaves deep wounds. These wounds extend beyond you, and ultimately infect your relationships.

So, if you lie to your boss, co-workers, neighbors and friends, you are no longer in a cherished, trusting relationship. People cease to be humans with souls and spirits to be honored. You have now crossed the threshold into a movie scene, where people are merely characters lined up for your own purposes. You have robbed yourself of the ability to share intimacy and authentic connection with someone you have lied to for your personal gains. You are assuming the person you are talking with cannot handle the truth, which is nonsense. As stated by Dr. Leaf, "A deceitful tongue is a dangerous road and creates false realities." Lying, if practiced regularly, will become deeply ingrained in your way of being and will alter your character and literally damage your brain.

Women of Principle, pause for a moment and take this next question seriously. Please don't be distracted by its simplicity.

What do you want? Really.

What do you want your one precious life to feel and look like? What do you want to experience in your day-to-day living? How do you want to feel in relationship with others? At your funeral, what is your legacy? How do you want to be remembered?

I propose the fundamental practice of simple honesty holds the key to achieving what you want.

Responsibility HAS POWER

Now that I have shared the neuroscience behind telling lies, as Women of Principle, we must take responsibility for creating brain damage in our own lives, while negatively impacting those to whom we lie.

If you are thinking, "Well, you don't understand my circumstance," or, "My white lies would never lead to this kind of exaggerated outcome," you may be right on both accounts. Your circumstances may be unique and require great courage to be honest, but God created you to live in truth by BEING an honest human being. No one was created to tell *any* kind of lies, no matter how small or seemingly inconsequential. It diminishes you, the receiver and everyone that is within the sound of your voice. And, for those of you who say that your white lies haven't brought you to drug addiction, adultery, losing a job or a dire consequence, I would reply with two comments. First, you are blessed with grace.

Secondly, your commitment to telling white lies isn't something you want to honor or defend. Remember, you are wonderfully and beautifully made. With God, your light will provide hope in your community. As it states in the book of Romans 12:2, "We are not to conform to this world, but be transformed by the renewing of our minds, that we may prove what is the good and acceptable and perfect will of God."

Honesty aligns with the will of God. The habit of telling white lies diminishes your authentic power and will create crippling divisions in your relationships.

In some cases, the power struggle and conflict will be obvious. However, in most cases, small white lies create invisible friction when someone's intuition speaks up and tells them, "This person cannot be trusted."

Human beings who live their lives embedded in a web of small white lies will carry the burden of a heavy soul and a conflicted spirit, whether they think it's evident or not.

I also look at the epidemic of white lies as a multiplier effect. Think about it. If every person in your office is telling small white lies, what is the short-term outcome and long-term impact on culture and the bottom line? Now multiply that effect a million times across your city and state. How can we live abundantly and create communities that thrive if the practice of simple honesty isn't a standard upheld by us all?

People who know my testimony often ask me how I re-created my life. Most have one of two responses: They are shocked that I lived through so many life-threatening, dramatic experiences and trauma without permanent physical damage to my body and a long-term negative impact on my mind, or they are wildly surprised that "someone like me" used to think and behave in such a radical, undisciplined way. I agree with both evaluations. I have looked back at the destructiveness of my past and have wondered the same thing.

SO, HOW DO YOU BEGIN TO
Embody Honesty?

*Here are a few important distinctions
that will empower you.*

1. **Steer clear** of those who practice gossip and lies. They will impact thought processes and overall well-being.

2. **Realize** that thinking is actually a practice. What and how we think will shape our ability to speak honestly. Take time every day to meditate and notice the 'what and how' of your thinking.

3. **Come** to understand that you have the power to observe your thoughts and choose what is honest, pure and noble. In order to win the spiritual war, God directs us to bring every thought captive. In other words, when tempted to embellish, pause, realize the thought is a defective interpretation and ask God for direction and the courage to speak honestly.

And, if you are in the habit of telling small white lies, exaggerating the truth for effect, omitting all or part of the truth or aligning with someone else you know is lying – today is the perfect day to start anew. None of us are perfect, and we can all easily fall prey. Still, like any bad habit or stronghold, we begin with forgiving ourselves for past self-destruction, take small steps and consistently make progress to living a life of honesty and authenticity.

PRACTICES TO BECOME A
WOMAN OF
Honesty

1. **Ask** yourself, What do you really want? Really connect with your deepest desires.

2. **Who** would you get to be in your life in order to live honestly, as a bold stand for love?

3. **Ask** yourself if telling white lies is a habit. If so, be honest. This is about living abundantly.

4. **Think** about your conversations over the past three days, and with no excuses, carefully examine any white lies you have told.

5. **Practice**, practice, practice being radically honest. Here is a simple technique: When someone asks you a question, pause. Remain quiet and think it through before answering honestly.

6. **Write** down your answers so you can be responsible for them. Without condemnation, say a prayer and ask God to remove any shame or guilt.

Principled Declaration:

Today, I choose honesty. I choose love and connection. I choose to examine my words before I speak and practice simple honesty. I am a Woman of Principle, and I accept my authentic power. I will trust God and lean on Him for the strength to practice honesty in all my affairs. I am responsible for being an honest woman. I will practice being honest for my own protection and for the honor and protection of those with whom God has entrusted me to be in relationship. I am free because I am an honest Woman of Principle.

2.

Becoming
IMPECCABLE
— THROUGH THE —
PRACTICE OF
BEING
YOUR
WORD

*"Use the power of your word in
the direction of truth and love."*

—MIGUEL ANGEL RUIZ

Dear Women of Principle, Know that you can:

- *Generate new results by keeping your word and honoring all your commitments.*

- *Reflect the characteristics of God by knowing the divine order of relationships.*

- *Live courageously by aligning your thoughts and actions.*

- *Understand the transforming power of language and use it to change the course of your life.*

Welcome to the journey of becoming impeccable with your word.

Brilliant Women of Principle, becoming impeccable with our word is a **bold stand for love.** Being known as a woman who is her word has influence and allows you to create meaningful relationships. Words have power. They are the window into who we are, what we believe in and how we treat others, and they provide a glimpse into our interpretations of the world. This practice builds upon the chapter of being honest.

As you practice this distinct way of living, you also become a member of a sacred community, whose leaders are dedicated to healing the world through honoring all people – from every walk of life – one word and one commitment at a time.

Those who have the discipline to practice being their word will shift every experience in their life and make a positive impact in the world.

As a community of women who live by a set of practices and principles, we come to understand there are supernatural characteristics and distinctions in the spiritual world of God that impact our ability to be impeccable with our word. As we dig deeper, I would like to first distinguish between the Word of God, language and the practice of being your word.

Across worldviews, religious traditions and spiritual practices, most people would agree that to speak is not only a divine privilege but a great responsibility. Since the beginning of time, priests and pastors, scientists, rabbis and life-long learners dedicated to understanding scriptures and sacred writings have offered their interpretations, practices and experiences around "the Word of God," the use of language and being your word. Despite their differences, the three are deeply connected.

Let me explain.

Understanding the Distinctions: The Word, Language and Being Your Word

The Word, designed by our Creator, is the most powerful force in the universe. It can include the Word of God as revealed in the Holy Bible or a Word of divine revelation spoken in your spirit directly or through prophetic utterance, as given by the Holy Spirit. The Word, in any form, is a creative force. The Word is God. Eternal. Timeless. Perfect. The alpha and the omega. The Word creates all things and is always in motion. The Word is holy.

Language

Another important distinction is between "The Word," eternal by its very essence, and our use of words in the human language. God gave us the gift of language to communicate and connect. The use of language is what makes us uniquely human and provides access points to spiritual truths. Language and your word choice have power. Language also has a vibration and energy, because each word spoken has an intention behind it. This means we use language to design our lives and influence every single person we talk with – every time we speak.

> *What we say to ourselves, in our minds or out loud, whether once or a thousand times, begins to shape and form in the world.*

What we choose to say matters a lot.

Being your word

How to be your word is at the heart of this practice and the center of the chapter. The final distinction is in the realization that our ability to master being our word and keeping our commitments is connected to our understanding of the power of The Word and our use of language. Understanding that the Creator, through His Word, generates all life and that language is a tool for connection, we can see the correlation. When we make a promise, it is generative. It puts something into motion. It creates an expectation in the receiver that we will be who we say we will be and do what we say we will do.

If you get nothing else out of this chapter, hear this one message:

> *If you master keeping your commitments — big and small — your life will radically transform, and all your relationships will elevate to a new level.*

The Influence of Language

As we are transforming from glory to glory into the image of God (2 Corinthians 3:18), we must know, at best, we will be able to imitate God's Word and be a reflection of His Spirit. His Word is perfect and always in motion. By using our language in a loving manner and doing our best to be impeccable with our words and commitments, we can mirror the love of God and have great influence on earth.

That's right. We have the power to influence everyone we meet. What we say matters. As we discussed, words have creative power. Words manifest experiences. Words have the power to bring people together in harmony and peace. Words also create wars, divide families and destroy reputations. The book of Genesis reminds us that, "In the beginning was The Word, The Word was God." According to scripture, God established life on this planet by using the creative power of His Word. Our Creator intentionally spoke man, the planets, moon and stars into existence. I am sure God's voice and word choice don't resemble our modern-day language, but, according to scripture, God did, in fact, speak the world into existence.

As children of this almighty and loving God, we, too, have been given the divine privilege of language, a power to create a world where all people can co-exist, living harmoniously and embracing diversity. It is possible. It may seem like an audacious claim based on the unbelievable examples of war, discrimination and mass destruction from the past, as well as some of the heartbreaking circumstances happening around us. Yet, we were created with the Spirit of love, power and a sound mind, which is the basis for peace between people and cultures. Once you know you have access to this kind of love, power and a sound mind, this knowledge serves as the catalyst for your own inner peace. It starts within you. Simply put, the transformation of your mind shifts your perceptions; it gives you a new outlook on life.

As you Become a Woman of Principle, you will practice speaking words of life, forgiveness and abundance.

What we say to ourselves begins
to take shape and form.

God tells us in the book of Proverbs 18:21 that life and death are in the tongue. Choosing life and honoring the life in others is a choice. You are not a robot. As Women of Principle, we become willing to be totally responsible for our lives and ALL our decisions.

It's a position of great possibility. It is also essential to understand the connection between thoughts, listening, speaking, choosing and words. Each is distinct from the other and yet they are interwoven, like a divine kaleidoscope. Each one impacts the other distinction and they all affect your ability and your willingness to be your word.

The power to do these things is in the *transforming mind*. This restoration and a newfound power will inspire a new choosing. You will choose to speak life over your children. Choose to pray blessings over your neighbor. Choose to pray for government officials. Choose to express gratitude for the small acts of kindness you receive throughout the day. Choose to speak loving words over your spouse and your ex-spouse. Choose to speak positively about your co-workers. Choose to bless your so-called enemies. You will choose silence over gossip. It feels like a stretch, I know. It takes compassion and a new wisdom to stand where pride, unforgiveness, fear and misunderstanding once stood.

Together as we master the practices in this book, we will evolve into higher levels of consciousness. We will become present to the impact we make on other people. We will take time to explore how thinking, speaking and listening impact our choices and the ability to be our word.

When more people of faith begin to understand the connection between God's Word, language and being our word, we step up into a kind of supernatural integrity, which is no longer a behavior but a way of being.

For the advanced seeker and learner reading the chapter, your light and wisdom is needed as part of the evolution of love. However, let's first master two aspects of Being Your Word. The first is to be responsible for keeping commitments. Secondly, we must understand the transforming power of language.

Thoughts + Language = Our Choices and Our Way of Being

Language and thoughts are connected. I realize this isn't a new idea. For the individual who has mastered this domain, welcome to the Women of Principle community. Your wisdom, learning and experience are a blessing to all us. Yet, until we all master this distinction and know this on a deep level, women cannot rise to their fullest potential. Many of us live our lives and do not directly connect thinking and language. Because both are aspects of being human, we simply accept them without understanding that they lead to *who* we become, *how* we show up in relationships and affect every moment of our lives. This includes our willingness to be impeccable with our word. Until we connect thinking and language, communities will suffer, and relationships will be strained. It is *time to rise* through the *transforming mind*; it is time to practice Being Your Word.

A Cat Named Sunshine

The first time I came to understand this practice on a deep level was during a leadership training. In this amazing training, a workshop designed around "Being Your Word" was central to my long-term breakthrough. A brilliant trainer named Barry shared an exercise that rocked a jam-packed room of adults by allowing us to experience the negative effects of not honoring our word. On the first evening, Barry read to the group the requirements to take part in the four-day leadership training. Included on the list were responsibilities, such as being on time, completing all assignments, no gum, and no drugs, smoking or alcohol during the four days. Seems easy, right? Well, day two proved otherwise. Class started at 5 p.m. Promptly, the doors opened, music played and people took their seats. The doors closed immediately at the start time, leaving a handful of classmates outside. Why? They arrived at 5:05.

As the doors re-opened, Barry asked, "Why were you late?" A laundry list of excuses came from the group, including traffic, work delays and stopped for food. He asked one of the ladies, "What is something or someone that is really important to you?" She responded, "My cat." Barry retorted, "What is your cat's name?" Her response, "Sunshine." Barry screamed, "If I told you that if you didn't arrive by 5 p.m. you would never see Sunshine again, would you have been late?" Her response, "Of course, I would have been here." Barry...

"Then why were you late FOR YOUR OWN LIFE? WHY DID YOU BREAK THE PROMISE YOU MADE TO YOURSELF AND EVERY PERSON IN THIS ROOM?

Where else do you show up late, breaking your promises in your life? Where else are you selling out on your life?" Shocked at his approach, she said, "It's not the same thing!" Barry yelled, "It is the same.

That's the problem. Your mind has been poisoned into thinking that you can keep your word whenever you feel like it.

You categorize the importance of being your word, while the rest of us pay the price for your broken commitments and lackadaisical attitude. Why would you keep your word for your cat and not for your own life? The entire training has been postponed because you and the others didn't keep your word. Your actions affect everyone — every day! What was more important to you than honoring your word?"

144

As tears rolled down her face, she remained silent; she realized Barry wasn't taking an argumentative position. **He was taking a stand for her life.**

Despite his perceived uncompromising demeanor, he wanted her to understand the connection between how we think about a thing, thus the comparison to the cat, and how that frame of thought impacts the words and actions that follow. This is the power of making and honoring our commitments. His message was for all of us in the training. This was his stand for all of us.

We spend our lives in a culture comfortable breaking promises and rationalizing the irresponsibility of it, without understanding the impact on our soul and the emotional well-being of others. We defend our smallness by making lame excuses. He reiterated every time we tell our children, spouses, co-workers, neighbors, family and friends we will do something, and we do not follow through – the gap between us grows wider. Intimacy suffers because the message we are sending is *something else was more important to me than keeping my commitment to you*. Then, we are too ashamed or too arrogant to take responsibility for our decisions, which expands the gap even wider. This is a vicious cycle.

Remember, you are loved, accepted and pre-destined for significance. There is a different path, where we honor our commitments.

Breaking our word makes the enemy very happy. The Word of God reminds us in 1 Timothy 6:12, "Fight the good fight of the faith [in the conflict with evil]; take hold of the eternal life to which you were called, and for which you made the good confession of faith in the presence of many witnesses." This is a reminder that being your word is a commitment and that your confession before witnesses means something in the eyes of God. The addictions human beings have to being right and looking good are so embedded in our culture that we would rather look good or take the so-called easy way out by not having a conversation about why we changed our commitments than humble ourselves and honor what we have confessed before witnesses, namely God.

In addition to sending mixed messages to others, the message we send to our own soul is that our word doesn't matter. Each time we tell ourselves that we will do something, and we don't do it, our word loses its strength. We no longer trust ourselves. It is a slow process that erodes our confidence, one broken promise at a time.

With courage and humility, think back over the last 48 hours of your own life. Are you impeccable with your word? If not, today is the perfect day to begin your courageous journey of living a transformed life as a Woman of Principle.

Add the practice of being your word
and keeping your commitments.

A Bridge to Intimacy

Culturally, we live in a world where we make plans and fail to follow through on the invitation. As parents, we tell our children we will pick them up from school at 3 p.m., yet we show up late to a concerned child who questions, "Where was mommy?" And we wonder why our kids have trust issues or deep resentments. We tell our workmates that we will give equal credit on a big business deal, and we end up taking full credit and getting the recognition, while leaving our partner disappointed and jeopardizing our integrity. We tell ourselves and others that breaking our commitments is no big deal.

Dear friends, every promise you keep impacts your relationships. Why? Because words are generative. When we make a promise, we create an expectation with the recipient. We build anticipation. When promises are made, people give their hearts away in expectation of something new emerging from the words spoken. Sparks fly when commitments are made. It is a sign of a new possibility.

According to scripture, the great call is to
"walk worthy of the calling"
(EPHESIANS).

To achieve this calling from God, our relationships must be in order. Scripture beautifully reminds us that true spiritual power flows from true obedience to the divine order of relationships and personal conduct. When we recognize that His Word is always in motion — and our words are always creating – we are more likely to be our word and keep our commitments.

The divine order is God, self, and others. Distinct *and* connected.

When we are impeccable with our words, we send the message, "You matter to me." When a commitment is broken or altered without having a conversation with someone, it creates confusion and distrust in the relationship. The gap grows wider.

On my own courageous journey towards being my word, I practiced keeping simple promises. This is my invitation to you as well. When I got sober, my first assignment from the therapist was to call my husband on the way home from work and ask if I could be of service. I did this simple act 260 times over one year. Often, he would ask me to do straightforward tasks such as run by the grocery store, Home Depot, pick up the dry-cleaning or run by the schoolyard and pick up our daughter, Mia. Each time we spoke was an opportunity to be impeccable with my word. It was the chance to generate a new context in my marriage. I did each task in excellence. Now, my word with him is solid. He trusts me implicitly. I am not perfect, and there are times I fail to keep all my commitments. The key is to take full responsibility immediately; explain why I broke the agreement and listen for feedback. It is critical we learn how to communicate effectively.

> *When we act in accordance with our commitments,*
> *we experience soul harmony.*

Women of Principle, this may sound simple, but don't underestimate the power of keeping commitments, big and small. As the light of God shines through your life, because we are all vessels of His light, people will watch you for inspiration and direction. Is there anyone in your life where you can practice keeping commitments in order to rebuild or expand trust? Where have you been incongruent with your words? There's no shame and condemnation – **this is a stand for your greatness as well.**

Being impeccable with our words and commitments in our world today is super important. At the core is a deep appreciation for all people. Being known as someone with an impeccable word means people can trust us to be kind and know that we will make every effort to keep our word. And, because we are perfectly imperfect, when we fail to meet our promises, we have the integrity to take responsibility without making excuses. What a relief to live with integrity.

Your Thoughts Link to Your Choices

Research shows that 75 to 90 percent of mental, physical and behavioral illness comes from one's thought life. According to Dr. Caroline Leaf, cognitive neuroscientists and author of "Switch on Your Brain," choice is real, and free will exists. Thoughts have physical matter in the brain.

With the practice of "renewing your mind" according to the Word of God, you can develop the skills to stand outside yourself, observe your own thinking, consult with God and change the negative, toxic thoughts to healthy positive ones instead. Philippians 4:8 tells us to think on "whatsoever things are of good report." When we begin to practice God First, our minds are renewed, and we can make better choices and keep our word. We become responsible for our language because we realize it holds divine power. With a healthy mind, our ability to honor The Word and be our word becomes more natural. In her book, "Switch on Your Brain," Dr. Leaf has proven that toxic thoughts and toxic choices change the wiring of your brain and throw your body into stress. This makes it harder to make good choices. This has always made sense, but now science proves it.

When you are tempted to gossip, speak harshly or tell white lies, take a deep breath and realize that your thought life is generating your language, which also impacts your practices and habits. Your choice of language is co-creating your life experiences.

Thoughts, words and choices are connected. When we allow this to sink in, and we choose to be responsible for 100 percent of our thoughts, words and choices, it has a transformative power to shift our beingness and our lives, forever. With self-awareness comes change.

In a world of emails, text messages and social media posts, sending hateful or shallow messages has become an easy way out. It is not an act of courage to dump vile words upon a co-worker, loved one or an acquaintance simply because they may have let you down, made a mistake or tried and failed. Being human can be challenging and as women living by Godly principles, learning how to show compassion and assume the best in someone is an act of grace. It aligns with imitating God. As Women of Principle, we must learn how to communicate well and be the bridge back towards connection with people.

Your Words Affect All Creation

Inspired by the distinctiveness and beauty of snowflakes, Japanese researcher Dr. Masaru Emoto spent decades studying the effects of prayer, music and intention on water, snowflakes and human interaction. Repeatedly, his studies proved that both positive and negative thoughts, words, and intentions had corresponding effects on the delicate crystalline structures, and ultimately, all creation.

When prayers and thoughts of love, kindness, or gratitude were focused on water, beautiful crystalline structures were formed. The same thing occurred while playing classical music. On the contrary, playing heavy metal music resulted in disjointed and distorted crystals. Similarly, writing words like, "You disgust me, "I hate you," or even "Adolph Hitler" on water containers caused the crystal structures to literally look sick. The structures go from light, well-formed structures to dark and distorted shapes.

According to Dr. Emoto, words carry the ability to either create or destroy. His scientific findings align with God's Word when he says that life and death are in the tongue. His message is simple, yet profound, as the vibration of words is explained as either having a positive or destructive effect on our world. He goes so far as to say the health of our water is a reflection of the human condition.

Now, consider the impact of your words and the collective conversations taking place in your family, your community and workplace. Our bodies are up to 60 percent water. What we say matters – a lot. If language affects the crystalline structures of water, how much more does what we say impact human beings? If a thought is toxic, it leads to equally toxic words and unhealthy choices. The mind and body become ill. Studies show communities that speak harshly and use more curse words have more crime. Remarkable, right? As confided in the previous chapters, the many poor choices I made throughout my journey of addiction all started with those toxic early thoughts of self-doubt and unworthiness. These thoughts were followed by words, "I am not good enough," "I am not smart," etc., which poisoned my ability to make healthy, wise choices later.

Now, think about a time when you walked into a speech, concert, sermon or conversation where the words spoken were powerful, life-altering words that expressed possibilities, opportunities for growth, supernatural blessings and words of encouragement. The vibration is electric. This kind of collective power and truth will cleanse your very soul, renew your mind and transform your way of being. Proverbs 23:7 reminds us, "As a man thinketh, so he is." Remember, as we practice God First, our minds and hearts are transformed, which gives us the ability to speak wisely – in grace and humility. As we change our thought life, we can live courageously and rise to our calling. Meditating on God's Word and spending time reading other life-giving books alter our perceptions, which affects our commitment to be our word. Science now shows that we are wired for love with a natural bias for optimism. With love, we begin to use the power of our words to edify, not condemn. As our mind becomes sound, our words reflect that transformation. Speaking against others no longer has the charge it once did. The rush of anger is no longer appealing because we now understand that every time we say something harmful, we literally affect the well-being of another child of God.

Being Your Word Develops You as a Leader

One of my favorite quotes for our Women of Principle community is from a book called, "Speak like a CEO" by Suzanne Bates. The entire book is about the secrets of developing the techniques and speaking skills for the voice of leadership. James Humes is quoted as saying . . .

"Every time you have to speak, you are auditioning for leadership."

This infers that people are always listening.

I love this simple quote. I have come to rely on this message to help me understand when to speak and when to listen. Becoming a Woman of Principle and a champion that others want to follow means developing a voice and a way of being that others trust. We learn to communicate well and keep our commitments. And, we develop ways of being, which reflect the principles and practices that define us. In Bates's book, 91.5 percent of the people she surveyed shared effective communication was a critical dimension in leadership. As part of the survey, participants voted the #1 value for leaders is honesty in *what they say and do*. This is evidence of the importance of being congruent with your word.

Becoming a Woman of Principle who leads is also about developing the ability to articulate a vision and inspire action, which means how we communicate and the ability to keep our commitments matter. Other important qualities include listening, giving feedback, emotional intelligence, knowledge and competence follow through and humility.

Women of Principle, this is an opportunity to develop your unique voice. Allow your soul to flourish. Be authentic. Developing our voices looks different for each of us.

Let me encourage you.

For the introverted woman, it is time to take a speaking role in a team meeting. Practice using your voice to build your confidence. Your voice and perspectives matter. For the woman who must "own the stage" out of the need to be noticed, it is time to sit quietly and listen for wisdom.

There is a time to speak and a time to listen. You are loved even when it is someone else's stage. For the woman who is the perfectionist or concerned with getting it right and says to herself, "Wait! Let someone else lead first to see how it's done." I say, raise your hand. Take a chance and be willing to get it half right. No matter which category you fit into, practice, practice, practice developing your voice.

The world is waiting for a strong, courageous woman whose aim is to be a servant leader and a lover of mankind.

In the words of award-winning poet, writer and speaker Maya Angelou, "At the end of the day, people won't remember what you said or did, they will remember how you made them feel."

Once your authentic voice emerges, there is no turning back.

Your true power is released. Speaking well of others will open doors and will give you options. No more complaining. No more gossip. No more making promises you don't intend to keep. You can do this!

Small Moments Matter the Most

Dr. Brene Brown, author, speaker and research professor at the University of Houston, who is also a woman of faith, was able to demonstrate through her research on trust, courage and vulnerability that trust is built in the small moments. These are small moments of transparency and honesty. Contrarily, trust is broken in what many of us may consider the small things. Gossiping is one example. Dr. Brown is quoted as saying, "A lot of times we share things that aren't ours to share, as a way to hotwire connection with a friend. You know what I call that? Common enemy intimacy." In other words, you haven't created an authentic connection by telling stories that aren't yours to tell, you are just fostering a false allegiance with someone over the gossip about another.

Gossip is defined as an abomination to God in scripture because it causes division.

Take this in, dear Women of Principle. Not with condemnation or guilt, but with a deep awareness that goes back to the start of this chapter.

Your word can create, destroy, edify or influence every single person, place and thing you come in contact with. You are a powerful woman of God.

No matter how small the moment may seem, being our word, day in and day out, is a compelling practice for Women of Principle. Remember, there are two aspects to the practice of being your word: first, understanding and being responsible for the transforming power of language, and, second, honoring and keeping your commitments.

Today, dear sisters, I encourage you to choose life. Choose to speak like you are loved

(JOHN 3:16), redeemed (ISAIAH 44:22)

and precious (ISAIAH 43:4) to God.

That's how you are described in the Word of God. Believing anything else and acting any other way will limit your dreams and devalue your life. Whether you encounter a CEO, bartender, airline pilot, student, or homeless person, interact in the spirit of love and generosity, being reminded that they too are precious in the eyes of God.

Once a word is spoken, it cannot be taken back.

PRACTICES TO BECOME
IMPECCABLE WITH
Your Word

1. ***Keep*** your commitments for 24 hours. When tempted to make a promise you know you cannot keep – pause and practice making commitments that align with your dreams, goals and aspirations.

2. ***Choose*** your words wisely today. Speak life over people. If you can't in the moment, pause, pray and make the choice to be silent instead of cruel.

3. ***Restrain*** from gossiping or complaining for 24 hours. When tempted to complain or gossip, take a deep breath, and again, choose silence. Say something kind ... anything!

4. ***Call*** and take full responsibility if you break a promise. Simply state, "I didn't keep my commitment, and I apologize." (Don't offer excuses, such as traffic, work or other business.) "I will do my best to keep my promises in the future." This statement narrows the gap and restores trust.

5. ***Remember*** the divine order of relationships. We are all connected. Knowing the Word will impact your language and your willingness to be impeccable with your words and commitments.

Principled Declaration:

Today, I choose to practice becoming impeccable with my words. I am a woman of great value, deeply loved by God. I am a woman who chooses to speak life and abundance over those I meet today and express kindness. I am a Woman of Principle, and I am accepted and precious in the eyes of God. So is everyone else I meet today. I will also practice being my word by keeping my promises and taking responsibility for all my choices. When I find myself thinking a negative thought – I am committed to turning it over to the Holy Spirit; I will pause before saying anything or taking action. I am a light in the world. Amen.

3.

Becoming GENEROUS
— THROUGH THE —
PRACTICE OF
SERVANT LEADERSHIP

"I have found that among its other benefits,
giving liberates the soul of the giver."

—DR. MAYA ANGELOU

Dear Women of Principle, Know that you are:

- *Brilliant and beautifully designed to reflect the heart of the Creator.*

- *Capable of living generously in heart, mind and hand.*

- *Wonderfully made and predestined to walk in love, light and wisdom.*

- *Attracting people to God by being generous with your life.*

Your unique fingerprint expresses the power and creativity of who you are and how your original genetic footprint can lovingly impact the world. There is only one you, and only you can bring your unique purpose to the world.

Practicing servant leadership is a bold stand for love.

However, most of us face a unique challenge. In our worldly thoughts, practices, speaking, listening and habits, we have forgotten our holy and divinely inspired destiny. For many, the light within you has been dimmed by devastating circumstances, challenging life conditions, harsh words diminishing your value, lies and half-truths you have expressed and your choice to align with false idols who seek to distract you from your true identity.

Many of us have adopted external interpretations of who we should be, which has created a false sense of self that is not aligned with your true purpose.

Keep the faith! Today is a new day! In the present day, you can choose a new path and come to understand the divine truths about your identity. We are all designed to live generously in mind, heart and hand.

Your power can be reignited to create incredible, breathtaking works of beauty in the world. Your works of beauty may be spectacular art painted on canvas, joyful sounds through a musical instrument or simply the expression of love and service in your daily life.

You, my dear sisters, are the way seers, the lamp upon the pedestal lighting the path for other women. You were created in love to imitate the life and love of Christ.

We were all created to express our unique God-given gifts and talents. We long to give our best. We are not created to hold back our gifts. It is unnatural. When we hold back our brilliance, we become unhappy and feel dissatisfied, which results in division and jealousy.

So, how can we create change, shifting towards our eternal purpose and ignite our brilliance? More importantly, how can we use our gifts to serve others? Service is about living beyond ourselves, connecting to our divine purpose and allowing ourselves to be a channel of God's love and intimate care for others. Service and being a generous person lights up the soul and transforms our mind.

When I made the commitment to live a life of love and sobriety, I recognized that I would have to overcome many self-limiting beliefs. I had a very low opinion of the life I had created, deep sadness about the time lost, and remorse for the deterioration in my relationships. The remedy I found for all of this self-focused thinking is serving others and living generously. I could later see clearly how self-centeredness, even when packaged as self-loathing or victimization, can itself be a form of addiction, or self-limiting behavior.

Honestly, at first, the practice of serving was still "me" focused. I wanted to be recognized for my "good works" and be viewed as a "good person." The pain and consequences of my addiction and the story I created about being deaf as a young girl created a void in my soul, and I thought being acknowledged by others for good works would somehow deposit in some imaginary bank of makeups for life screw-ups or fill this gap. It doesn't. Looking towards others or their affirmation of you to fill a void only creates a larger gap.

The divine practice of service is the reward.

Even Jesus came to serve. He washed the feet of his disciples to demonstrate His love for them. Although Jesus walked on water, restored the sight of a blind man and could raise Lazarus from the dead, he served.

As I practiced service and the principle of generosity, the "me" focus inexplicably shifted, and I Became a Woman of Principle who enjoyed practicing servant leadership and service – simply for the act of walking in love and imitating God. The need for approval and recognition slowly disappeared as I connected to the holy principle of service. The gaps were filled with a spirit of generosity, joy, kindness and gratitude.

I love the simple scripture in John 3:30,

"He must become greater; I must become less."

My dearest Women of Principle, as you begin to serve, you will learn to give for the sole purpose of giving. As we learn to serve for the sake of giving, our hearts are open wide to miracles, signs and wonders. As we learn to serve others, we become soft and pliable. We see human beings in a miraculous way. Their perceived faults dissolve and their inner beauty appears. The people we viewed as broken become holy and complete. We realize they, too, have been created to be servant leaders. People we sought approval from simply become comrades along the journey of light, and we become partners in humble service. The book of Matthew has a beautiful scripture that reminds us, "You are the light of the world. A city that is set on a hill cannot be hidden. Nor do they light a lamp and put it under a basket, but on a lampstand, and it gives light to all who are in the house. Let your light shine before men, that they may see your good works and glorify your Father in heaven."

Through service, we begin to see humanity through the lens of the Holy Spirit. Our minds transform, and our hearts open wide. The power to live courageously returns.

As a trainer proficient in transformational distinctions, I have spent the past few years sharing powerful lessons with women who are in recovery. I am in my calling with women who are seekers, those who have journeyed through hell and have managed to survive and thrive. The ladies come from all walks of life. Their past struggles range from drug and alcohol abuse to divorce, homelessness, low self-worth, loss of a career, a false sense of grandiosity, sexual trauma or many forms of neglect. I am not clinically trained, so I don't make clinical assessments or provide any medical diagnoses. However, because I am transforming and living courageously by grace for God's glory, *I am a stand* for what is possible for them. I am rising to my call, so I know what is possible for them. Despite their perceived failures, broken hearts and disappointments, there is a beautiful masterpiece (Ephesians 2:20) underneath it all. My commitment is to poke holes in the lies of the enemy, so the light of God shines through.

Here is the humbling truth, according to The Hayford Bible Handbook, *"God's joy is to confound the adversary by displaying His glorious power through those He has rescued from hopelessness and restored to kingdom partnership in Christ."*

Exhale.

Because I have practiced serving others quietly for more than 21 years, the practice of service has transformed into the principle of generosity and servant leadership in my life. I've learned that serving others is an act of imitating God. Serving others is fulfilling the command to "walk in love" (Eph. 5:1). There are many truly amazing servant leaders who have inspired me, such as Bettie Spruill, Ray Blanchard, John Maxwell, Simon T. Bailey, Maya Angelo, Pastor Julie Mullins, and Martin Luther King. However, most of the people who inspire me most are the incredible servant leaders who would be known as everyday people, yet they have the same passion for important issues such as equality, education and health and wellbeing. These incredible leaders have inspired me to use all of the gifts and talents bestowed upon me to make the world a healthier place for all. For more than a decade, mentors, family and friends have encouraged me to move past the selfish, but real concern of what people may say about my past and rise to the calling upon my life, which is to share the victory of the journey through hell.

The story is simply a tool to relate to the challenges you may be facing. It is to let you know that you are always loved, never alone and there is a profound calling upon your life.

I now understand my gifts do not belong to me. I am only a vessel for Him to reach others. There is nothing amazing about me, per se. It is God working in and through me that is worth recognizing.

In the book of Luke 6:38, Jesus shares the principle of generosity. "Give and it will be given to you: good measure, pressed down, shaken together, and running over will be put into your bosom. For with the same measure that you use, it will be measured back to you." My dearest sisters, as we learn to give openly in heart, hand and mind, with no expectations of receiving in return, the spiritual principle is activated in a way that can never be measured by man. Becoming a Woman of Principle who serves others generously debunks the myth of scarcity. We come to understand there is enough of everything: love, friendship, food, career opportunities and anything you can imagine.

At Christ Fellowship, John Maxwell gave a sermon sharing there are two kinds of people in the world: those who lift and those who lean. I encourage you to think about who you want to be in the world. Lifting others is about the practice of servant leadership and aligning with the principle of generosity. Scripture is clear that we are to have fervent love for one another.

Love heals and lifts all to their full potential. Remember, you are amazing, creative, intelligent and worthy. The Bible tells us . . .

"God is within her, she will not fall; God will help her at break of day."

(PS. 46:5)

PRACTICES TO BECOME
A WOMAN OF
Service

1. ***Practice*** having an open hand and heart by giving the gifts of time, talent, money to those in need. And, don't mention your acts of service to anyone.

2. ***Think*** about who those you can serve. How can you add value to your family, place of work or community? Pick one area and serve without seeking validation. The Holy Spirit will honor you.

3. ***Say YES*** to service without knowing all the details. Servant leadership will not always be convenient.

4. ***Thank God*** every morning for new beginnings. Take a moment before your feet hit the floor to make conscious contact with the Creator.

5. ***Be Honest.*** If you are still in the "me" zone, it's okay. Transforming our minds is a daily practice.

Principled Declaration:

Today, I choose to replace my focus on me with an intentional commitment to the service of others. I am a Woman of Principle who seeks out opportunities to serve with humility, gratefulness and love. I will practice sharing the best of my brilliance, gifts and wisdom gained from my transformational journey to live beyond myself and connect to my divine purpose, allowing others to do the same.

4.

Becoming
VICTORIOUS
— THROUGH THE —
PRACTICE OF
RUNNING
WITH
CHAMPIONS

"You were made to release your brilliance. If you're not releasing your brilliance, igniting your creativity, or being a game changer where you work, move on. Do something else."

—SIMON T. BAILEY

Dear Women of Principle, Know that you can:

- *Generate love in the world, because you are victorious, confident champions.*

- *Live an abundant life abounding in fullness of joy and strength of mind, body and soul.*

- *Embody the principles of truth by sticking close to other leaders who are running the race with purpose.*

- *Discover your calling and rise to your full potential by running with champions.*

- *Release your brilliance, be a champion and contribute to the world stage.*

You, my dear sisters, have a source of power eternal in nature, which will not only transform your life but the life of everyone you meet. And, as this chapter unveils the importance of running with champions, you will come to understand and be responsible for how you use this power. This knowledge and the decisions and actions that follow will directly impact the world, as purposed for your life. Becoming victorious through running with champions is a **bold stand for love.**

I will introduce the distinction of power through divine revelations and the practice of running with champions, thus, becoming a champion that others want to follow. This practice is an amazing journey where you will humbly discover blind spots, build strengths, develop skills and challenge limiting beliefs, all while creating relationships that illuminate your heart and renew your mind. There is a process to running with champions where one discovers this power and how to use it. My transformative journey began with seeking respected mentors, pursuing friendships and becoming a mentor. It is through this practice that I have come to know my true identity and God's intended use of our power, as well as the joy of running with spiritual champions who bring light and wisdom to others.

Discovering our True Identity

We all seek an identity. The root of our identity will dramatically influence our systems of thought, our beliefs, and ultimately, the choices we make. When we discover that God is who He says he is — and we place God First and train like champions, praying, meditating, worshipping and reading the Word of God — our worldly identity shifts. We are filled with the Spirit of God, and we claim, "We are more than conquerors in Christ." The human heart and mind on their own are incapable of grasping the dimension of who we are in Him. It is through the Holy Spirit that we come to align with our true identity. Champions embody the principles of truth by sticking close to other leaders who are running the race with purpose.

Champions call out the greatness in others, recognizing that God's call is for everyone. Women of Principle, you are called to release all false identities that limit your ability to live abundantly.

We Are One

Because we have adopted limiting self-beliefs, use language in ways that diminish possibilities and have been taught that we are separate from our fellow man, we have come to believe stories that we are separate beings. We tell ourselves that I am "other" than you. This separateness causes discord and war, which manifests in the soul, spirit and body and has a deep impact on each of the tripartite. As Women of Principle, we must come to understand that we are one body in Christ. The ego and that little voice in our head tell us that it is okay to dehumanize people who don't look like us and have differing opinions. This small voice of ego also gives us permission to harshly judge people and gives us permission to be character assassins, based on their actions and behaviors. We are fully convinced that we have the right to judge them and condemn them because of their differing worldviews or mistakes. Respectfully, I would say that we have all fallen short of the glory of God. Extending grace becomes possible as our identity is rooted in what the Word of God says about us.

If I may, allow me to present another perspective that saved my life and will provide wisdom, humility and right use of God-given power. This understanding will position you as the champion God has called you to be.

Power in the Word of God has several definitions to describe its divine use. One of four words used in scripture to define power is exousia, (ex-oo-see-ah), which means the authority or right to act, ability, privilege. Jesus had the exousia to forgive sin, heal sickness and cast out devils. In the Bible, Jesus gave his followers the exousia (i.e., ability, right, privilege) to preach, teach, heal and deliver, and that power has never been rescinded (John 14:12).

As Women of Principle, this is exceptionally important.

Today, we have the same power. Although we are not one of the 12 disciples, by definition, Jesus gave all his followers incredible power, and we must come to understand the dynamics of our power in order to use it properly. On an individual level, we are sometimes tempted to misuse power to control other people and outcomes. Often this is driven by 100 forms of fear, including the fear of losing what we have and not getting what we need. Collectively, we go to war in the name of God. We create social groups, neighborhoods and board rooms that only allow certain people in; every race, creed and religion has participated in this kind of intentional division. Then, we stand and proclaim, "Equality for all!" We demand justice, and yet in our own lives, we are demeaning the very nature of human life by name-calling and ridiculing. We have come to believe that if the person has political or faith-based views "other" than ours, that it gives us permission to name call and belittle their opinions. It is nonsense. Peace cannot be created through divisive words. Period.

Language supernaturally manifests results in the world based on our words and intentions. Sarcasm isn't peace, and it is not a characteristic of a champion.

Whenever you are confronted with an opponent, conquer him with love. Stay true to your course. Mahatma Gandhi stated it brilliantly when he said, "The day the power of love overrules the love of power, the world will know peace." Gandhi is a champion.

I once used the power of language to rip into a mentor who was sternly telling me what to do during an intensive nine-month leadership experience. Although his goal was to push me beyond the old stories that kept me from consistently having an extraordinary life, my ego railed against him. It shouted, "You cannot tell me what to do! I don't work for you, and I don't give a shit what you think!"

Silence was returned.

My ego raised up in opposition. I used force, and I meant to push him away. It was my way of saying, "I am uncomfortable with your request; I don't know how to share my viewpoint gracefully, so back off!" Once we ended the call, I knew an apology was the appropriate action. Yet, I didn't apologize for two months. I allowed my pride to keep me from having a loving connection. It wasn't until we had a final leadership exercise around the distinction between "Godly power and worldly force" that I realized how my behavior may have harmed him. I humbly approached him, asking for forgiveness. I admitted that, at the time, I choose to "be right" over being in relationship. He gracefully and quietly leaned towards me, whispering, "M.K., you are a powerful woman. Don't apologize for your power; it was given to you by God. You have the supernatural ability to teach, heal and inspire. The goal for every human being is to learn the distinction between self-centered force and the right use of power *and* how to use power in a way that honors everyone." My heart melted with gratitude for his grace. We both cried and embraced as friends for life. His forgiveness stays with me, even today. I use this experience of running with a champion to remind me that we are all saved by grace. Because he offered me this gift, I have turned towards others and extended the same kind of exousia.

Women of Principle, when people at work or in the community selfishly try to use their positional power to gossip and divide teams, which is usually aimed at hurting reputations, we must learn how to step out of ego and into our divine leadership position, serving others by extending Godly direction, grace and forgiveness.

Our response is critical because we become what we practice.
Our lives begin to reflect the practices we embody.

My mentor and dear friend Bettie Spruill would say, "You are what you do."

Over time, I have learned how to listen to the concerns of others, align my response by trying to answer their true concern. Then I speak with language that brings the team back together. Where I used to want to be right, I now aim for peace and unity. I have used many of Dr. Brene Brown's techniques from her book, *Dare to Lead, Brave Work, Tough Conversations and Whole Hearts* to teach me what daring leadership looks like in the face of great challenges. Champions pay it forward and realize when harsh words are spoken, force cannot create peace. Remember, giving a piece of your mind is never worth peace of mind. The power to act rightly comes from the Spirit of God and the practice of leading and following others with respect.

Your source is holy. The very breath that is within each one of us is "the breath of God." The Bible is clear that our lives are infused with the energy of God, the Creator, the almighty and eternal consciousness. This energy lives within each human being and flows vibrantly every day. We are living, breathing, organic beings. In some deep and profound way, we are all connected.

In a blog article authored by Dr. Caroline Leaf in September 2019, she explains, "A 'me, myself and I' mentality tends to distort our perspectives and values, impacting the way we see and interact with those around us and setting up negative feedback loops in the brain that affect our overall health and wellbeing."

Champions are well aware of this fact.

Whether you choose to acknowledge and claim responsibility for your power or not, it is there. The opportunity before you, my dear sisters, is to not only own your power, but to choose to harness the power in a way that aligns with your life purpose. The question is: How can you harness your power in a way that generates more love and less suffering? How is your use of power affecting those around you? Is it a spirit of love, control, competition, jealousy or humility? As you become open to learning this skill, you will exude the spirit of kindness and equity will be possible for all human life. This transformative journey begins within you.

Our world has many inspirational examples of influential pastors, scientists, educators, medical doctors, coaches, peacemakers and theologians who have used their influence, training, education and wisdom to improve the planet and life for all mankind. Thought leaders from many backgrounds and worldviews, such as Mahatma Gandhi, Dr. Deepak Chopra, Dr. Brene Brown, Dr. Caroline Leaf, Dr. Timothy Keller,

Bettie Spruill, Dr. John Maxwell and my very own senior Pastors Todd and Julie Mullens, are excellent examples of diverse spiritual giants with a variety of spiritual gifts and talents. They are champions in their respective fields who have been given glimpses of great truths about God and the scientific mysteries of the universe. However, the greatest teacher and ultimate champion in my own life is the example of Jesus Christ. In my own journey becoming a champion, I have practiced mimicking the life of Jesus. For many years, I have practiced thinking upon whatever is true, whatever is noble, whatever is just, whatever is pure, whatever is lovely, whatever is commendable, and praiseworthy (Philippians 4:8), as a way of transforming into the champion I was created to be and attracting the same in my life.

Jesus' life is the ultimate example of using supernatural power rightly to heal, teach, preach and demonstrate what is possible when our lives align with God's purpose. He created a tribe of followers, which, despite their imperfections, became very impactful champions.

These everyday champions have a supreme
purpose – and so do you!

Breakdowns Lead to Breakthroughs

Our first inclination when searching our soul and discovering we have been running with individuals who do not align with our dreams is to wince in shame and make excuses. Yet, even successful executives, working in reputable organizations, who by worldly standards look like they are kicking butt, can come to the realization that despite their material successes, they have compromised their values. My invitation for you, dear sisters, is to count yourselves blessed if the Holy Spirit or a champion has shone a light on an area of your life and rebuked a thought process or behavior. Let me share my own story.

My angelic friend Julie Cotton, once my mentor in the master's course at a nationally recognized leadership training, taught me a valuable lesson. There was an intense leadership exercise that included a feedback session, designed to stretch worldviews and poke holes in faulty beliefs and interpretations so the light of God can shine through. The training is to introduce the distinction of "blind spots." But, because of some unhealed wounds, I still carried shame; I interpreted feedback as harsh criticism. In my heart of hearts, I believed the only way to make up for my old ways of being was to strive towards perfection. My aim was to be perceived by others as "the best" at everything: sobriety, spirituality, business and any activity that would "prove" that I was worthy of love and friendship. It was exhausting. I earnestly believed that if I was perfect, I would be well-liked. But what I failed to understand is there is no freedom in striving for perfectionism, only deep resentments and more shame. Identity-based perfectionism prevents intimacy and connection. Its focus is on controlling outcomes, looking good and being right. However, I honestly didn't see myself this way or realize this character defect at the time.

During the four-month leadership exercise, I got feedback, which not only hurt my feelings, it downright pissed me off. Yet, Julie provided a context that shifted my life forever. She explained, "Mary Katherine, God is only about love, truth and humility. He loves us all so much that when we are out of alignment with those characteristics, He allows people in our lives to provide feedback for us to realign with God-centered principles. Instead of feeling shame, explore the experience with gratitude. Be in the question of what you can learn from the feedback and make the changes that align with the vision you have for your life of purpose. Leave the rest to the Holy Spirit to interpret for you."

Boom! Breakdown and breakthrough! My old mindset vanished like vapor in the wind. I received and accepted the Spirit of Truth. I came to understand the Holy Spirit appears as the power by which we are brought to faith and that helps us understand our walk with God. By His wisdom,

He brings a person to new birth, new revelations and a new spirit. The Holy Spirit is the helper given to us as a gift and brings the world under the conviction of sin, righteousness and judgment back home into right relationship with God. Because I was running with champions, I received a supernatural gift of honesty. I now know that perfectionism isn't a quality a Woman of Principle seeks to achieve. And, I came to see that when I receive feedback, it means my mentors care about my long-term success and are willing to share their experience and divine revelations while in relationship with me. This disclosure includes what they may see as positive attributes, as well as qualities they want me to consider changing in order to live my best life. And so, it will be with you, my dear sisters, when you are led to the right champions to run with.

Your understanding of the distinct connection between breakdown and breakthrough will impact how you run with champions; it will impact *how* you will lead, follow, and the tribe you will attract and run with in critical times.

Stick with the Winners

Early in sobriety, I realized the importance of running with champions. In the program, we simply state, "Stick with the winners." The practice of sticking with the winners isn't simply a phrase that sounds good in conversation. When it comes to relationships, we are greatly influenced — whether we like it or not — by those closest to us. It affects our way of thinking, habits, speaking, listening, and our decisions. Of course, everyone is unique, but research has shown that our environment affects us deeply. Many studies demonstrate we are the sum of the five people we share the most time with daily. Vivian Zayas, a professor of Psychology at Cornell University, conducted a series of studies examining the impact of close relationships on our perceptions. There were many complex findings, but in summary, the studies proved that there is often a subconscious transference of attitudes, thoughts and perceptions from those we are in closest relationship with.

While it's ideal to be closely surrounded by positive, supportive people who want you to succeed, it's also necessary to have your critics. What I have learned from Dr. Brene Brown is that constructive criticism leads to mastery, whether or not the person delivering the message is skilled at providing feedback. According to a study in the Journal of Consumer Research, "Tell Me What I Did Wrong: Experts Seek and Respond to Negative Feedback," novices prefer positive feedback, but experts want negative feedback so that they can make progress. This certainly lines up with my own journey in becoming a woman with the courage to live as a Woman of Principle. How about you? Are you open to feedback that may be hard to hear and do you invite these relationships into your life?

Mile 25

One of my life's dreams was to be a triathlete. The problem is that every time I dive into the ocean beyond 10 feet deep, the theme song from the movie, *Jaws*, echoes in my mind. So, instead, I turned to long-distance cycling – by accident. When I was working at the American Heart Association, I held a position that allowed me to roam the halls of hospitals, interacting with top donors who secured funding for heart research. During one of my visits inside a large heart hospital, a very tall, looming man named Kevin walked up to me and leaned in to ask, "M.K., do you want to join my cycling team? We are building a group called Storm Riders, and I want you to consider being on the team." I loved the idea and agreed to participate. I bought my expensive bike, all the gear and began riding feverishly with Kevin and the entire team. Riding with experienced cyclists who were champions in the sport taught me many valuable lessons on my journey to Becoming a Woman of Principle.

One afternoon I told Kevin, "I want to be an excellent rider, so what do I need to do?" Kevin's response, "Go ride your bike!" That was it. That is all he said, as he turned and walked away. So, that's what I did for the next several years. I began riding my bike almost every day. I rode alone; I rode with groups, large and small. I spent hundreds of hours riding my bike, in the sun, wind, rain and heat. I trained for thousands of miles, and I "became" a cyclist. It was grueling and rewarding work.

I recall one ride early in my journey that illustrates the value of running with champions. About 30 of us met in Juno Beach, Florida, and the goal was to ride 50 miles. It would be my first 50-mile ride. I felt pretty good as I arrived that morning, socializing with my peers.

Every rider on the team was more experienced than me. We had rain and excessive winds, and I had a tough time keeping up with the group. One of the key practices I learned from running with champions is the practice of leading and following while being a contribution to the team. One of the rules of cycling with a team is that each cyclist does their part and spends time in the front of the pack, "pulling" the long line of riders behind you. As the lead rider, you stay in the front position for a few miles, then fall to the back. It is a rotation. The idea is that as the lead rider, you build physical and mental strength by pulling the group. You earn your place on the team, and the rest of the group gets to leverage the momentum of drafting before it's their turn to pull the pack of riders. Eventually, my time came to pull. I still remember the road, winding along A1A's open roads, along the beaches, through many neighborhoods with the strong winds at my face. It was demanding and overwhelming. I knew this exercise would exhaust my physical resources; however, I aimed to do my part. It was an act of courage to stay in place as the lead and not immediately roll to the back of the pack, because I knew the experienced riders would be critiquing my skills.

In previous rides, Kevin wouldn't allow me to pull, because I wasn't ready. In addition to pulling the group, there is a true champion-like role in this exercise. The leader is always on high alert, looking for roadblocks, potholes, traffic and other obstacles that could harm the entire group. The front rider is in a position of trust. The lead rider must know the signs to alert the teammates behind him or her of any danger quickly without jeopardizing the safety of the team. I was proud that I had earned my way towards the front of the group. I held my position for several miles, before stepping left and allowing the next man up to lead the way. As I pulled left and let up on the momentum, I felt a pat on my back, and the rider behind me shared, "Good work, M.K. Welcome to the team." A moment of gratitude. All my hours of cycling prepared me for this day. I felt like a contributor to the group, and I smiled as many of my teammates shouted words of encouragement as they rapidly pedaled past me. I took my position as the last rider so that I could rest and prepare myself to lead again, as we circled the halfway mark. But what happens next taught me even more about the value of running with champions.

As I mentioned, I was the newest member and least-experienced rider in the pack. As the ride progressed, I grew weaker and more exhausted. Pulling the group several times that morning depleted my energy. However, there was no going back. We were 25 miles into the ride, and there was only one way home – I told myself to keep pedaling, breathe deeply and keep your head in the game. Kevin saw me struggling, so he offered me a hand – literally. The huge, 6'3" giant, placed his hand on the small of my back and pushed me for several miles. This was exemplary leadership. He was leveraging his strength, giving me a chance to recover, and he was demonstrating his commitment to my performance. However, once he realized that I couldn't keep up with the group and that this too, was part of my growth, he looked at me and said, "M.K., I know you want to be a great cyclist, so I am going to allow you to earn your stripes. See you back at camp." Then, slowly, he pulled away from me, and he took the lead position in the front of the group; they accelerated, and before I could count to 50, they were gone.

Over the next 20 miles, I experienced a range of emotions, including anger, exhaustion, hunger and physical pain. My mind wondered from, "What in the hell am I doing out here in the rain and wind?" to "I hate this stupid sport," to gently encouraging myself to remember, *"I am capable of getting back to my car one mile at a time."* That day, not only did I become a better rider, I became a healthier human being. The struggle and perseverance were part of my transformation to become a stronger rider and a Woman of Principle. The only way to become a better rider was to practice the ride. The way to become a woman who perseveres with integrity in the face of great challenges is to repeat the practice of running with champions and the actions, until the practice becomes a principle ingrained in your way of being. Running with champions trains us to become a trusted leader and teammate.

As I approached the 50-mile marker, I could see a small group of my team cheering me on, "You can do it, M.K., keep pedaling." They waited for me. My heart experienced profound joy on many levels. I earned the respect of my fellow riders, which is important in a team environment, and I wholeheartedly believed for the first time in many years that I am a strong, powerful, authentic woman. That was my first day of many 50-, 75- and 100-mile rides. Running with champions and having mentors that model healthy behaviors and demonstrate unique leadership and team-based qualities is important. So, choose wisely!

Women of Principle, what is your own dream? What do you want to accomplish in your own life? Who do you dare to become? And, who are your champions? If that little small voice, called your ego, tells you that you don't have what it takes to achieve a dream, be still and know that He is God. You were marvelously made. You are perfectly imperfect. Now get up and get moving! Move towards your dreams by aligning yourself with other champions. My dear friend and mentor Simon T. Bailey states it brilliantly, "In order to accomplish your goals, you must be willing to take the first step and begin 'walking in the direction' of your dreams."

When you face your own wind and rain in life, remember, you have the courage to complete the task at hand, in excellence. Just watch your confidence emerge. Along the way, the Spirit of Love is faithful. He will provide nuggets of truth and the courage to achieve your own 50-mile goal.

Who is Your Tribe?

So, in the pursuit of champions, you will discover the abundance of friendship. This section of the book is heartfelt. If I am honest, all I have ever wanted is to be in connection with diverse women who are deeply passionate about making the world a better place for everyone. There are so many other women who feel the same way; we yearn for settings and relationships that generate joy, laughter and peace. However, culture tells us we must have it all together, so we hide our shortcomings and imperfections, which prevents the intimacy that comes with an honest friendship.

Although I have occasionally struggled feeling like the outsider looking in, most of my life I have been blessed with having rich friendships with some remarkable women. These are female warriors who take a stand for those without a voice, who despite their own concerns and imperfections, leverage their passion and create the space for others to thrive. This tribe of women is what I missed the most during my battle with addiction. Addiction's goal is to kill, steal and destroy. The enemy's weapon is isolation, where the spirit of fear screams outrageous lies, which causes more separation, anxiety, depression and confusion. Addiction prevents intimacy. In the program, we describe this journey as "jails, institutions and death."

Despite my dreams and the deep love I had for my career, friends and family, I was dying – literally. My addiction was winning. My healthy mind was a distant memory. The dreams as a young executive working in broadcast media seemed like impossible aspirations. I desperately wanted to be beautiful again; I desired a strong body, beautiful mind and loving nature. I missed evenings congregating with my lady friends, where there was groovy music, dancing, great meals, and storytelling echoed in the hallways of my home. So, when I received the miracle of a renewed mind and a healthy body, I prayed earnestly to reconnect with the girlfriends I love and female mentors who demonstrate the balance between vulnerability and strength. The other true blessing – God did for me what I could not do for myself – through my new life, there is a new generation of incredible women who I found both in and out of the program.

Other super talented women in recovery, although anonymous in their program, band together by linking hearts and becoming one voice in sobriety.

Our return to self-worth is a testimony of God's wondrous grace, the power of transformation and the abundance that comes with running with champions.

The same is true for the many other addictions and strongholds some of us face – addictions to food, the affirmation of others, the feeling of love or unhealthy romantic relationships, emotional dependence, work, money, and the list goes on.

Women of Principle, who are the members of your tribe? Who are the 'core five' driving you towards excellence and emphasizing that discipline and consistency are critical to living your best life? Who is taking an eternal stand for your life?

RUNNING WITH LADY FRIENDS
WHO EXEMPLIFY GRACE THROUGH
IMPERFECTION INSPIRES US ALL TO

Be Champions.

PRACTICES TO
RUN WITH
Champions

1. ***Identify*** your own 50-mile goal. Write down one bold goal for your life and begin taking the steps towards manifesting your dreams.

2. ***Stick with the winners!*** List the champion(s) who may coach you towards achieving that goal.

3. ***Examine*** your tribe! Who are the five people you spend the most time around? Do they think and act like champions? If so, ask them for Godly counsel and honest feedback. Be open, not defensive to what you learn about how you show up.

4. ***Be a champion.*** Who can you serve by sharing your story, being a servant leader and extending the love of Christ?

Principled Declaration:

Today, I choose to run with champions and explore the blessings of servant leadership and divine relationship. I choose the spirit of generosity in my heart, and I will lend a hand to those in need without the need for recognition. I am a woman of power, and I lead by example. I believe I am selfless, blameless and chosen, and I will practice joining myself with other leaders who think and act like champions in every area of their life. Today I am open to being someone's champion so they, too, can rise to their calling.

5.

Becoming
WISE
—— THROUGH THE ——
PRACTICE OF
GOD
FIRST

*"He is First above all rule and authority –
and He alone is worthy of the number one
position in our lives."*

—(DEUTERONOMY 6:4)

Dear Women of Principle, Know that you can:

- *Love God with your whole soul and spirit and put Him first in all things, every day.*
- *Choose how you will be in relationship with the Creator and others.*
- *Set your priorities in order to create the life you desire.*
- *Manifest your dreams and transform your relationships by putting God first.*

By putting God first, everything else is automatically set in divine order. This chapter will help you more clearly define your values and set your priorities to elevate the mind, body and spirit, according to God's purposed plan for your life.

Putting God first is a bold stand for love.

You are a divine child of God. You were created to love God with your whole soul and spirit. Our souls, dear sisters, make us uniquely human. It is where our self-consciousness lives. Biblically, the soul is the intellect, will and emotions. This powerful component of being human gives us the power to reason, make choices and choose *how* we will be in relationship with the Creator and everyone we encounter during our journey on earth. At the core, the spirit of man is where our God-consciousness resides. Deep inside each of us, tied to our spirit-man, is where our faith, hope and love is fed by the Word of God and nurtured by the Holy Spirit.

The Word of God urges us to practice God First by stating, "You shall love the Lord your God with all your heart and with all your soul and with all your mind. This is the great and first commandment." (Matthew 22: 37-40) Yet, despite our divine nature, most of us are motivated by selfish desires. Although our hearts long to love and be loved by God and others, when our priorities are out of order, creating the life of our dreams will be challenging.

Understanding the distinction between the body, soul and spirit is critical as Women of Principle. The New Testament reveals human nature as tripartite: spirit, soul and body. Knowing how God created each structure, divinely inspired, will provide insights and wisdom. This wisdom will give you the ability to use your power wisely. Used in humility, this power can transform your life, impact your community, and, most importantly, align your will to God's.

Therefore, God First is fundamental to living our best lives. God First is a beautiful practice that transforms all three of these amazing aspects of being a physical and spiritual being. All the dreams you store in your heart, daydream about as you walk slowly along the ocean shore or write about in your journal become a reality. With God First, your dreams manifest and your relationships transform. God First creates a love language that changes you from the inside out. People will be attracted to you because your connection rests in the One who has the ultimate light and eternal power to heal, recreate or expand your life. You will be transformed by grace, able to live courageously as a Woman of Principle.

Now, hear my heart clearly. Your life doesn't have to be a total mess to reinvent your future. You may have a fantastic life with meaningful relationships and a dynamic career. I pray you do. Regardless, I encourage you to lean into the practices within God First and allow the Holy Spirit to impart wisdom, which will elevate the mind, body and spirit.

I realize God First can be a challenging commitment. Despite my love of the Holy Spirit, as soon as I'm awake and have made a conscious connection with God, my next inclination is to hop out of bed, rush to the coffee pot, feed the dogs, hug my husband and check my emails. I mean, let's face it, the ego tells us that we are so important that we must get up, get out and get moving. Can you relate?

However, the spirit of God tells us to . . .

"Be Still and Know that He is God."

(PSALM 46:10)

Becoming a Woman of Principle comes down to knowing your values, setting your priorities and having the courage and discipline to practice your values. Your values evolve into living by rock-solid principles. These principles help to guide your journey and alter your ways of being.

When I reflect back to the darkest days of my life, being deaf as a little girl and being an addict as a young woman, these are the most obvious experiences where my broken heart, shattered dreams, chaotic mind and wild ambition demonstrate the need for God and direction in my life. It is natural when life presents a crisis to shout out, "God, please help me!" Tragedy and pain have a way of bringing us to our knees, which is a profound way to discover the peace and love of our Creator. However, as we grow in our walk with God, having a daily practice produces a profound connection with the Holy Spirit and we discover our divine significance.

Most people tell me putting God First is challenging, because they cannot sit still. I can relate. Can you? When I started practicing putting God First, my brain was on fire. I had a hard time sitting for five minutes without being distracted. I would read a page in a daily prayer book or the Bible, and I couldn't recall what was on the page, let alone pray about the content or apply it to my life. Maybe I am the exception, but my experience tells me otherwise. After mentoring dozens of women over 21 years and leading thousands of women as a transformational trainer, an absence of a God First practice is always at the core of misunderstanding of their value. Most women I know have struggled to achieve their worth through the disease to please – searching for meaning in people, places and things.

But the good news is that, without exception, when the four elements of God First are applied to everyday living – prayer, meditation, praise and worship, and study – relief can be immediate.

GOD IS

faithful.

When we take just one step towards Him, His presence and eternal wisdom renew our mind and change how we interpret the circumstances of our lives.

As a Woman of Principle, this step of placing God First is the opportunity to practice humility and discipline. Let's start by taking a simple approach in each area of the four elements of God First.

Prayer

Prayer is simply communication with God. Because God is personal, every person can offer prayer. The most meaningful prayer comes from your heart. For me, prayer is the most intimate way to learn to trust other people. Because of my past trauma, when I am in a stressful situation, I can still suffer from detachment and distrust. Without prayer, I can become guarded. I have come a long way, but often, my first emotion is anxiety and my initial reactions are to back away from people. So, prayer was and still is a precious tool to stay connected to God and the people in my life. It is a beautiful exercise to send supernatural love and well-being towards people. The generous act of praying for others releases supernatural outcomes that we cannot even fathom. Consistently practicing prayer has given me the chance to stay connected to the source in every situation – whether peaceful or stressful.

I was 14 years sober when I had an emotional setback, suffering the side effects of my pent-up trauma. One afternoon my boss shared information with me at work that caused me great concern, because it was not true. Even though I knew it was based on water-cooler chatter, I allowed it to create intense concern in my soul. I became intensely focused on two old character defects, **perform-to-win and prove myself.** Once those defects of character were activated, I became laser-focused on demonstrating that I deserved to be on the team.

According to my therapist, this reaction is based on being deaf as a little girl. When schoolmates told me that I wasn't part of the group, not welcomed, or would make fun of how I talked, I discovered two ways to prove my worth. It was then that I became conditioned to perform to win and prove myself. Sometimes, even now as a Woman of Principle, the subliminal message of not fitting in can still spark a deep wound and character defect. The spirit of rejection is the weapon the enemy uses to throw us back into isolation and self-reliance.

What a big mistake! Because worthiness is a gift from God and cannot be earned, when we try to earn worthiness, we create more division and chaos in our relationships. Character defects push people away because we are stepping out of our divine nature and into a performance-driven relationship. The enemy wants us to believe that we are not worthy, and the spirit of the enemy is looking to kill, steal and destroy our peace of mind, our reputation and our relationships. Worthiness is an innate gift from God and cannot be accomplished through temporary gains, such as winning a prize, getting a promotion at work, purchasing an expensive car, new home or any other material item. Worthiness just *is*.

As we practice God First, our sense of worthiness returns, and we feel less compelled to defend our character. When we trust in God, we step back into alignment with supernatural laws, our vibration shifts, and then miracles happen. My God First practice saved my peace of mind, restored my relationships at work, created a dream job and a trusting relationship with my boss. I learned to sit, pray and know that the Holy Spirit was orchestrating every move, each conversation, and all I had to do was practice praying with humility and discipline. The amazing power of this practice is we come to know that God is a God of transformation – mind, body and soul. All who come to Him in prayer, even those who we perceive as our enemies or adversaries, are being transformed through our prayers.

For three months, every day, I prayed for each person with whom I worked. My prayers focused on them experiencing abundance, love and connection. Prayer changed my soul (i.e., concerns, emotions, thoughts) and supernaturally affected each person that I daily placed back in God's hands. With this simple act of obedience, I was transforming with each day of prayer into humility and wisdom.

Do you get it?

BECOMING IS A

transcendent

EXPERIENCE.

As we pray, we become more like the image of God. Our souls are forever altered, and our spirit-man is evolving into the very essence of faith, hope and love. It says so in the Bible.

Women of Principle, I wish you a profound practice of prayer that creates unity through humility. The Bible states . . .

"*Let nothing be done through selfish ambition or conceit, but in lowliness of mind let each esteem others better than himself.*"

(PHILIPPIAN'S 2:3)

Praise and Worship

Praise and worship is an act of acknowledgment by which the virtues or deeds of another are recognized or extolled. Praise and worship through music have been an influential bridge to God in my life. Out of all the God First practices, I have experienced God's amazing grace, healing, love and supernatural transformation through musical praise and worship. Godly music creates a vibration that literally transforms the spirit and soul. Collectively, when large groups come together and welcome the Holy Spirit into praise and worship time, miracles abound. Light enters the dark hearts of man and transformation takes place. Scripture reminds us, "Where two or more are gathered, I am with you." (Matthew 18:20)

In my darkest days as a teenager with a serious hearing impairment and a young woman desperately fighting to overcome the throes of addiction, worshipping God through music was my lifeline. It gave me some relief from despair and loneliness. I clung to worship music like I needed oxygen to breathe. And, during other vulnerable times, I have leaned on music to continue to transform my soul and strengthen my God-consciousness.

Most recently, my dad was diagnosed with a rare autoimmune disease. The coughing, fever and extreme fatigue lasted months while the doctors tried to find the cause in order to diagnose him. By the time they determined the disease, it was too late.

I will never forget the moment the team of physicians, residents and nurses walked into his room. The collection of white jackets spread across the hospital room, as my dad laid in bed. My mom and I clutched hands and walked near my dad; the three of us gripped onto one another. We knew by the look on their faces, the news wasn't good. We braced for what came next. The lead physician delicately sat at the foot of my dad's bed and said, "Mr. Sabol, we have a diagnosis for you. You have a rare autoimmune disease called Good Pastures, which is extremely rare and very dangerous. Most patients live for five years. Many doctors will go their entire career and never meet a patient with Good Pastures. The disease has attacked your lungs and kidneys, and we need to begin an aggressive treatment to save your life. Unfortunately, your kidneys will never work again, and we will do our best to save your lung function." Silence.

My dad's face went from disbelief to profound sadness. His heart was immediately broken, as tears welled up in his eyes. He looked over his right shoulder towards mom and me, hoping to find relief from the pain and surprise of such devastating news. Tears rolled down his cheeks as he tilted his chin towards his chest to try and catch his breath. The room went silent, waiting for him to look up.

Moments later, a medical resident with a warm disposition made his way through the sea of white coats, gently walked towards my father, and softly whispered, "Mr. Sabol, you have my personal commitment. I will do everything I can to take care of you." Dad wept. The other residents in training held back their tears, and yet, their compassion was palpable. One by one, they reached for my dad, to try and comfort him. Slowly, the medical team left the room, along with my mom.

I sat on my father's bed, and our eyes locked. He looked at me, wiped a tear from his right cheek, and quietly shared, "All these years, I was caught up in the rat race. My priorities, in many cases, were out of alignment. I wasted days worrying about things that don't matter. I promised your mother that we would travel and enjoy our time together. Now, I am very sick, and I cannot go anywhere." In that very moment, my life forever changed. Our hearts became one, as he looked to me for comfort. We held hands, cried and tried to find some relief, as we sat in the cold, sterile hospital room. The man who once went into drug-infested neighborhoods to rescue me was now looking to me to rescue him.

Because of my transformed heart and life, my dad trusted me in his most vulnerable moment. He was attempting to grapple with the most difficult news he had ever received. "Five years", he said. "That's not a very long time." I was able to provide hope in a very challenging moment, because I was prayed-up and the times spent previously in private praise and worship gave me the ability to be present and intimate with my dad in such a way that gave him courage for his future and assurance that Almighty God would give us the strength to get through this situation.

For 38 days during his first round in the hospital, we took one day at a time. Each morning at 6:30 a.m., we prayed and listened to worship music. Despite the challenges, circumstances and physical evidence, we believed in a miracle. We cited scripture, asked friends to join us in prayer and supplication and walked by faith. Despite many tough days, critical setbacks, more days in the hospital, and over 500 dialysis treatments, we finally got our miracle. It took three years of standing in faith, singing songs, praying in the spirit and trudging the road to happy destiny; yet, by the grace of God, the miracle manifested.

Practicing God First will give you the courage to stand gracefully and boldly in the face of great challenges. I know as Women of Principle, you too, have stories of overcoming great obstacles. Thanks to God First, I have witnessed women triumph over situations that seem impossible with grace and humility. It doesn't mean we don't experience intense feelings when challenges arise. It simply means that because we practice praise and worship, we have God First as our strength.

On a lighter note, praise and worship is also the choice to rejoice on the good days. Your praise is powerful. It is an invitation for God to inhabit your mind, spirit and body. Praise opens the door to joy in the morning, joy in the evening and joy all day long. Turning up the music shifts your perspective and changes the atmosphere. The Bible says, "Draw near to God and He will draw near to you." (James 4:8) Today's worship music is so magnificent that it can purify your heart, while instilling the Word of God. Each morning after my quiet time, I turn up the music. It's like a concert. My home is filled with the Spirit of God each morning, because we welcome Him into our hearts, minds and home.

You're also invited to welcome the Holy Spirit into your life. Rejoice over the millions of blessings you have received in your lifetime. Celebrate your breath, your eyesight, hearing, taste, touch, emotional connections to your beautiful children and spouse. Recall everything and anything you have ever received and count it twice. All gifts have come from God. Due to advances in neuroscience, researchers can actually measure how listening to and playing music affects the brain. Research has shown that listening to uplifting music boosts brain chemicals, which lifts your mood and lowers stress. This simple act increases the neurotransmitter dopamine. Dopamine is the brain's "motivation molecule" and an integral part of your pleasure-reward system. So, throw on some praise and worship tunes, and according to neuroscientists, get smarter, happier and more productive. More importantly, give God all the glory and all the praise while you listen.

Consequences of Worshipping Idols

In today's culture, praise and worship of idols is an epidemic, but one subtly camouflaged. We are strongly encouraged to use social media platforms such as Facebook, Instagram, Twitter and YouTube to idolize the accomplishments of celebrities, movie stars, politicians, talk show hosts, entrepreneurs and those with bright ideas. On another level of self-will running riot, we also have come to idolize ourselves by over-posting selfies, while embellishing our travels and daily activities to impress our audience. In some cases, Facebook and other social media platforms have taught us to be a society driven by superficial "likes" and "loves."

Can you relate? As Women of Principle, we can commit to striking a balance between sharing our appreciation for individuals doing amazing work and crossing the line into worshipping someone you admire. Always be aware of the subtle camouflages.

In the first of the Ten Commandments, God prohibits idolatry . . .

> "I am the Lord your God ... you shall have
>
> no other gods before me"
>
> (EXODUS 20:2-3)

The command asserts that we will either worship God or something else. Notice, it does not envision a third option — there is no possibility of our worshipping *nothing*. We need to worship something, because that's how we are created. We cannot eliminate God without creating God-substitutes. Something will capture our hearts and imaginations, becoming the most important concern, value, or allegiance in our lives. So, every personality, community, and thought will be based on either God Himself or on some God-substitute, an idol.

It may seem like a *duh* moment to you, but think about the 400 million daily social media posts. The ads promoting fast, expensive cars, handbags or Jimmy Choo shoes are harmless, until we begin to worship these items, connecting them to our worthiness and finding our inherent value in them.

Have you ever posted anything with the hope that a certain person would see your post and like your page, offer an interesting comment or share your brilliant ideas? These are examples of worshipping false idols. I am not judging. I am simply stating the facts. We've all done it.

So, to break the ice and practice the principle of honesty, I will go first and tell you that my disease to please at various times in my life created a worshipping effect. In the early 2000s, I had a mentor named Jack Hand. He was a wise old man when I met him and astute in the ways of the world. He told me, "Mary Katherine, your core problem is you put people on pedestals and no one other than God belongs on the throne." Because of years telling myself the story of not being good enough, I put people who appear to have it all together on "the throne". Their opinions of me were of supreme importance, and I would behave in ways that I thought would impress them; as a result, losing my authenticity. My source of strength and the focus of my praise and worship was in the wrong direction.

The irony is that idolizing anyone, regardless of who they are, only creates division. Why? Because it goes against the supernatural laws that God put in place. Only God is deserving of praise. As stated by the great Tim Keller, "If anything becomes more fundamental than God to your happiness, meaning in life and identity, then it is an idol." C. S. Lewis is quoted as saying, "I pray because I cannot help myself. I pray because I am helpless. I pray because the need flows out of me all the time – waking and sleeping. It does not change God; it changes me." When we place people on a pedestal, we lose our principled perspective and rob ourselves of the chance to be forever changed by intimacy with our Father. We become unbalanced, and our relationships become twisted.

Women of Principle, may your only idol be the Holy Spirit and your praise be to Jesus Christ.

Meditation

Meditation is the practice of reflection or contemplation. Meditation is a lost art for Christians, but the practice needs to be cultivated again. This form of meditation is not to be confused with either the cultish or practice of mindless abandonment or focused mind control. For Women of Principle, the meditation I want to reinforce is best described as *waiting on God and thinking on His Word and His love.*

Once more, this is a God First approach that changed my whole life. I mentioned earlier that my mind was on fire, racing from thought to thought. I remember driving down the highway one afternoon and calling my mentor, Stephanie. I cried out for help because my brain was running at speeds that I could not control. I felt overwhelmed by the busyness of my mind. The effects from the drugs made things much worse in early sobriety, but even with long-time sobriety, without the God First principle, I can suffer from misaligned priorities. In my 21 years in the program, I have overcome other dependencies, such as being busy, working too much, and perfectionism.

Many other women who don't suffer with a drug habit still have an agonizing mindset that is consumed with addictions. Can you relate to addictions such as social status, greed, gossip, jealousy, control, power, shopping, spending, selfish or lustful desires, among others? If so, thank God we are more than conquerors through Christ Jesus.

As you read earlier in my testimony, I struggled with a hearing impairment and was caught up in an addictive lifestyle. As I fought for my life, I knew meditating on God's Word and creating a supernatural mantra would save my life and prevent me from going crazy. Today, as a Woman of Principle, this practice keeps me centered.

One of my staple scriptures, 2 Timothy 1:7, "For God did not give me the spirit of fear; but the spirit of love, the spirit of power and the spirit of a sound mind." Even in the everyday practice as a Woman of Principle, I use the Word of God as a tool in my meditative practice. When I go to my hot yoga classes on Saturday mornings and the instructor asks the class to choose an intention, word or phrase for the session, I always choose a phrase like, "Love, Power and a Sound Mind". Other times I focus on a short scripture like Philippians 4:13, "I can do all things through Christ", or I ask the Holy Spirit to speak to me for wisdom and humility, which are my two greatest requests from God. Dear sisters, there are so many beautiful scriptures for you to meditate upon for your own practice.

I have received amazing messages from the Holy Spirit. When I take the time on a regular basis to wait on God and to be in the position to hear his voice, messages of hope, rebuke and direction have come from the Holy Spirit. In my meditative practice, the Spirit will bring a face or name into my mind with a direct command to *forgive, release, or let go*. Messages on life direction also come to me when waiting on God becomes a regular practice. As you spend time studying the Word of God, the Lord will bring wisdom into your consciousness by bringing a word from the Bible, a sermon, book or song directly to your mind. He is so faithful. All we must do is take small, meaningful steps to know Him, and He intimately shows up in our lives.

I am most grateful that I developed a consistent practice of meditation. It took years to be able to sit quietly for long periods, but the rigorous practice has paid off. I look forward to Saturday mornings when I know I have 90 minutes with the Creator.

Let me make myself clear, though. I don't meditate just to get a word, phrase or direction from God. For me, the principle God First, is a way of life where I have come to simply want to be close to Him and in His presence, because I have come to understand He is "I am". He is the alpha and the omega, the beginning and the end, the first, the last and ever-present. When I am quiet, I have come to know that He is ever-present. He is consciousness, which is always present. When I am still, developing a deep knowing about Him is a gift.

As a Woman of Principle, if you are fearful, meditate day and night on 2 Timothy 1:7; if you have a restless heart, meditate on peace, using the simple word, shalom as your mantra during your meditation. God takes great delight in the shalom, the wholeness of your total well-being. He will meet you where you are, my dear sister.

My dear Women of Principle, I wish you a restorative practice.
Peace to you always.

The Word of God

In meditating and studying the Word of God, you will *know* God for who He is and will be transformed in five powerful ways by:

1. **Surrendering** self-focused perspectives for the supernatural wisdom of God.

2. **Becoming** aware of and ridding yourself of toxic thoughts.

3. **Releasing** old stories and belief systems and reframing your narrative according to God's Word.

4. **Living** up to your true purpose and position in Christ.

5. **Increasing** your desire to discover God and be in His presence.

Finally, the Word of God, as profoundly explained by Jack W. Hayford:

Each time a person picks up the Bible, he or she opens the grandest message ever given to earth. Nothing has ever come to the hands of humankind that even approaches the completeness and clarity or the love and grace presented in God's Word. Exceeding any of its other superlative qualities is the Bible's unique, multi-dimensional power. The Bible breathes with truth that is proven in its power to set human beings free. The Bible transforms individual men and women trapped in any and every order of human failure, lifting them from selfishness and sin to dignity and destiny by the power of the grace it reveals. And the Bible heals the human soul through its unparalleled ability to communicate and infuse love into and through human nature by the power of the Holy Spirit.

Sigh! I love this description of the Bible's purpose. It warms my heart to know there is hope for everyone. The Bible, and the journey of transformation has been a long and winding road. Out of all the God First practices — meditation, prayer, praise and worship, and the Word of God

— establishing this practice was and continues to be a stretch for me. Like with so many others, reading the Word of God takes discipline, because the power and wisdom of scripture doesn't always jump off the page for me. It often leads me to asking more questions than I have answers.

Although truth, grace and love abound in the Word of God, I, like many others, can misunderstand the heart of God, because I read the Bible through the lens of self-limiting beliefs, bruised life experiences, toxic thoughts and cultural influences. Coming to understand the Word has taken time and the instruction of prophetic leaders and pastors. I have come to understand God's ultimate plan is to bring humanity (me and you) into renewed relationship and active partnership with Him. This renewed relationship is based on trust and position, as well as being responsible for how we activate and use this power given to us by God.

I agree with Jack Hayward when he states, "the quickest summary of the Bible's message might be made with a three-word outline: revelation, redemption and restoration." Because I am not a theologian and my goal is not to try and convert anyone, per se. I want to be clear about my intention for this section of God First. My aim is to invite you into your *own* conversation with God; using these three areas as an outline for transformation, living courageously and rising to your fullest potential.

Allow me to use this framework to try and share my own experience within these three areas.

Revelation.

How can we know God is real? This is one of the most profound questions we can ask as human beings.

The definition of revelation is, "the divine or supernatural disclosure to humans." Like an author writing a book, the only way a character in a book could ever know there was an *author*, is IF the author writes himself into the narrative and introduces himself as the author. In Genesis, God created Adam and Eve. God *introduced* himself to Adam. They built a relationship. Then, Adam asked the author of all creation to add a new character into the story of humanity, which God *created* and Adam *named*, Eve. And, so the story goes.

The Word of God is the most powerful, mind-blowing revelation that God is. In order for our finite minds to know of God and to understand Him in any way, God must take the initiative by introducing himself to us. The revelation power of God is found throughout scripture. The Holy Bible is God's way of giving mankind an inside look into the character and love of the Creator. Because God is relational, He provided the stories, spiritual laws and guidelines, which give us a way to connect to His plans and design for living. As we spend time renewing our minds in the Word of God, *He discloses himself to us.* That's how we know God is who He says he is.

In my own journey, reading the Word opened my heart, and I came to see patterns of how God wrote himself into my story a long time ago. In fact, scripture continues to shape my worldview and change my mind, allowing me the opportunity to continue transforming into the same image from glory to glory, just as by the Spirit of the Lord (2 Corinthians 3:18). In other words, the revelation of God is a process. Knowing Him takes discipline, but He is faithful to reveal himself and His wisdom as we take time to sit and "Know He is God."

Redemption.

Redemption is the story of love. In the program of recovery, we would phrase it as, "God is doing for us, what we can never do for ourselves."

Understanding how redemption works and defining the Word is important. By definition, redemption means "deliverance and setting free." You may be asking, "Deliverance from what?" Another excellent question.

When Adam and Eve sinned and chose to believe the lies of the enemy instead of trusting God, the first original sin entered into the world. Up until that day, Adam and Eve stood in perfect relationship with God. They used their free will to obey God's commands and did not eat from the Tree of Knowledge. The moment they chose to walk in self-will and sin against God, redemptive power was introduced into the relationship between God and man.

Although there were consequences for their sin, God immediately began to repair the relationship. Their decision to follow the serpent and give in to temptation has affected billions of people. That's how sin works. It is passed down from generation to generation in a variety of ways. Since that day, we all sin and fall short of the glory of God. But there is hope. This is the good news of redemption. God sent the perfect man, Jesus, to teach us who God is, His design for living and the way to peace. Jesus restores the unity between man and God.

Scripture also provides a moral compass for us to compare and contrast our lives. As we read the Bible, we can practice honest self-reflection. Until we can admit that life isn't working, or that we are not living our best lives, we cannot see the need to make changes, let alone the importance of being in right standing with God. We don't have to be a hardcore addict, liar, cheat or thief to atone for our character defects. As we mature in our walk with God, regular atonement for our sins can include habits that are more socially acceptable, such as white lies, control, obsession with self, resentments, anger and jealousy.

Redemption is *the* ultimate promise that we are loved by God. He reaches out to us repeatedly. Christ is the bridge to grace, eternal life, wisdom and power. This bridge gives us access to the Holy Spirit. All we need is an open mind, which swings open the gates of Heaven – right now. This is not a performance-based journey, Women of Principle; this is grace.

Another word used to describe redemption is atonement. I am always amazed how Jack Hayward and other scholars get to the heart of the matter by breaking this word down into three profound parts: at-one-ment.

Through redemption, we are one with God.

Restoration.

On the journey of becoming a Woman of Principle, this scriptural theme is integral to our long-term impact. Simply defined, restoration is a "return to God." I also like to refer to it as "the journey home."

No matter our past, God is calling us to rise to our full potential by returning to Him. Like many other heroes in scripture, you are called to make a positive impact in the world. Some Women of Principle will be called to large arenas, board rooms, foreign lands, and will be catapulted to the stage where the limelight will be yours. However, most of us are called to a seemingly less glamorous, but equally important mission. It is where the day-to-day impact is made throughout the world. This approach is what I like to call "the stealth approach." This is a thoughtful and careful approach to living a transforming life, where courage and humility is our commitment.

We, the everyday woman, have received the restorative power of grace, and we are committed to sharing our transformation through the message of our lives. Day in and day out, we apply simple practices that attract others to the *becoming* of our story. This *becoming* encourages other women to seek God. Your grace and gratitude for your rising to the call upon your life inspire others to put God First. In my old life, although I was raised in a Christ-centered, faith-based household, I lived like a woman who never knew Christ. I worshipped the golden calf of money, career titles and popularity to fill my soul.

During that time, I didn't live in the freedom that God intended. I lived bound to my own desires and hindrances. I lived a life of repression and mistaken identity. I lived the life other people wanted for me. I lived a life under *systems of thought* based on lies and deceit. The truth of God was never in me in such a way that I could defend my mind against external influences. I failed to know the Word, which limited my wisdom and connection to the Spirit of God. I lived on tenacity and the willfulness to achieve my goals. Anyone relate?

It wasn't until I willingly turned towards God, *returning to Him*, that I could live courageously. Like many women, the greatest gift I have ever received is being set free from the bondage of self. Rejection, pride, abuse, fear, shame and anger no longer control me. I pray your God First practice removes any of the ties that keep you from truly exploring and experiencing what is possible in your life.

The three supernatural themes of scripture — revelation, redemption and restoration — have the power to cut loose the heavy burdens we carry when we go it alone. In other words, having a God First practice and knowing God matters in every aspect of our lives.

It will affect how you live your life, the condition of your heart and your ability to forgive and Rise!

PRACTICES TO
BECOME A WOMAN OF

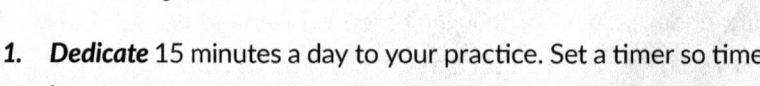

1. **Dedicate** 15 minutes a day to your practice. Set a timer so time is not a concern.

2. **Pick** one of the four areas to begin your God First practice: prayer, meditation, praise & worship and study of the Word.

3. **Seek** out a Woman of Principle whom you admire and who practices God First in her own life. Ask her to mentor your journey.

4. **Enjoy** getting to know God. It is YOUR time to rise to the full potential of your call.

Principled Declaration:

Today, I choose to put God First in every area of my life. I am a Woman of Principle inspired by grace. I strive to live a life that reflects the heart of God. I am perfectly imperfect, and yet, I am loved by

God. I have access to the Holy Spirit through prayer, meditation, praise and worship, and study of the Word. I am loved, accepted and I am pre-destined to rise to my fullest potential by living a courageous life.

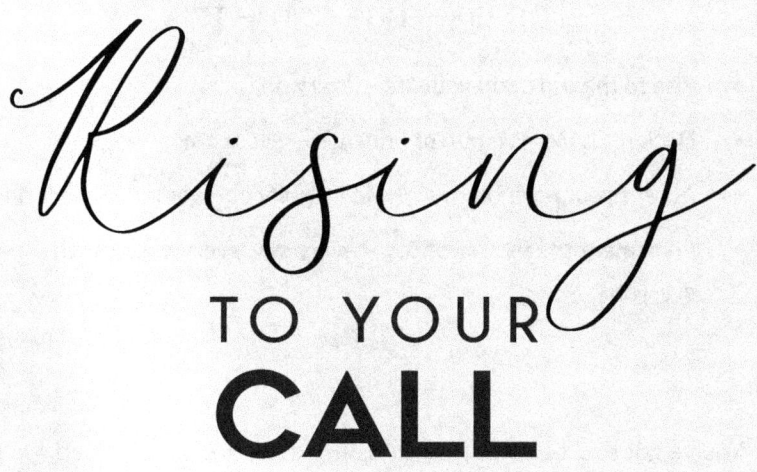

Rising
TO YOUR
CALL

LIVING EVERY DAY AS A
WOMAN OF
PRINCIPLE

"Your transforming life is a mark of God's radical love over your life. We are all Transforming. Living. Rising."

—MARY KATHERINE MORALES

Dear Women of Principle,
The time has come to:

- *Rise to the call upon your life — every day.*
- *Declare "I AM" Woman of Principle — every day.*
- *Accept your position as a divinely significant woman — every day.*
- *Implement the five practices — every day, everywhere, with everyone.*

You've got this, beautiful lady! As our hearts are transformed, we rise from failures — big and small — to success and divine significance.

What We Practice, We Become

Up until this point, we have focused on the practices of Becoming Woman of Principle. Why? Because what we practice, we become.

This simple phrase holds the key to your 2.0 life.

Practices take a certain kind of commitment that shapes *who* we become and *how* we live our lives.

Every practice in this book has God-infused principles that transcend time. Each practice has the power to profoundly change your soul and your heart for humanity. We can accelerate the process by coming to understand only love will prevail in the end. Still, our ability to experience heaven on Earth is unequivocally connected to recognizing there is a divine order in the universe. As we choose the Spirit of Love over dishonesty, self-centeredness and false idols, our ability to solve the world's most pressing problems will be possible. You play a vital role in the movement of God — right now on Earth.

You BECOME a bold stand for love the moment you commit to the practices and use the principles as your guide.

Although there are several principles you can choose that relate to each practice, I will give you one primary principle for each practice to guide your new journey. As your Godly wisdom expands, other principles will also be important.

Worth Repeating

Principles are fundamental doctrines upon which beliefs and morals are formed. Principles are timeless and help us to determine our values when we face challenging circumstances. The distinction between a value and a principle is that a principle is a guide for behavior, not beliefs. So, it is less *about what you believe* and more about *trusting in the guiding principle.* They are the base you stand upon as you live as a Woman of Principle — every day. This may seem odd, but remember, God's thoughts are higher than our thoughts. Sometimes our belief systems will be tainted based on life experiences, so we must learn to lean on principles that guide us through complicated relationships and conversations.

IMPLEMENTING EVERYDAY *Principles:*

A STAND FOR LOVE

The *Practice:*
HONESTY.

The *Principle:*
TRANSPARENCY.

Honesty:

A bold stand for love. Adhering to the facts. Not embellishing.

Transparency:

Openness. Clarity. Simplicity.

Outcome:

Freedom. Authenticity. Joy.

Commitment:

The commitment to transparency guides our behaviors, words and choices. We focus on the strength of transparency when tempted to embellish. The practice of honesty creates more openness and clarity of mind. We choose simplicity as a way of communicating and connecting with others. As Women of Principle, we become a reflection of God's light as transparency becomes our guiding principle. We honor the light in others by accepting honesty as a way of being.

The *Practice:*

BE YOUR WORD.

The *Principle:*

IMPECCABLE.

Be Your Word:

A bold stand for love. Keeping commitments and being responsible for the power of language.

Impeccable:

Faultless. Pure.

Outcome:

Powerful. Reliable. Trustworthy. At Peace.

Commitment:

Impeccability guides all decisions. When tempted to misuse our power or break promises, we focus on the principle of impeccability. We accept our influence and creative energy as a gift from God. As we practice being our word, the principle of impeccability aligns with wisdom, which is no longer a behavior but a way of being. With practice, we become impeccable, Women of Principle.

The *Practice:*
RUNNING WITH CHAMPIONS.

The *Principle:*
VICTORIOUS.

Running with Champions:

A bold stand for love. Discovering blind spots, building strengths, developing skills, renewing your mind and becoming a leader.

Victorious:

Abundant. Confident. Loved.

Outcome:

Trusted leader. Teammate. Friend.

Commitment:

Knowing we are already victorious guides our thoughts and actions. We are abundant. We stand in confidently with nothing to prove. We humbly recognize, through Christ, we are champions and evince moral harmony. We align our strengths with other leaders. As Women of Principle, we understand the significance of having mentors, becoming a mentor, running with champions, creating a tribe and becoming a leader.

The *Practice:*
SERVANT LEADERSHIP.

The *Principle:*
GENEROSITY.

Servant Leadership:

A bold stand for love. Living beyond ourselves, connecting to divine purpose and serving others.

Generosity:

To give freely.

Outcome:

Passionate love. Abundance. Reflecting Jesus's heart.

Commitment:

The principle of generosity is our North Star as we serve, knowing service liberates the soul. We appreciate the universal principle, "give, and it will be given to you," as an opportunity for all people to have an abundant life. Through servant leadership, radical generosity becomes our stand for love in the world. As Women of Principle, we serve because Jesus did, too.

The *Practice:*

GOD FIRST.

The *Principle:*

WISDOM.

God First:

An eternal stand for love. Recognizing with God First, everything else falls into divine order.

Wisdom:

A supernatural "knowing" that can only come through the Word of God, scriptures and whispers of the Holy Spirit, also known as the Spirit of Love.

Outcome:

Wise. Walk in humility.

Commitment:

The principle of wisdom becomes our true inspiration. The practice of putting God first gives us a glimpse of who God is through prayer, meditation, praise and worship, and the Word of God. We come to know God is a God of transformations — mind, body and soul. All who come are transforming from glory to glory into the image of God through the spirit of the Lord. As Women of Principle, we point everyone towards God First. Wisdom comes from the Creator.

I know that if you are applying the five practices and aim to have the principles as your North Star, you are experiencing challenges in your thought processes and belief systems. They are designed to challenge limited perspectives and world views. However, they will transform your mind, expand your heart and give you access to the spirit of God, who is transforming us from glory to glory into the image of God. Your transforming life is the mark of God's unconditional love upon your life. His love refines our character, and we rise to the call upon our lives with a shared purpose, to point all women towards God. Why? His spirit reveals the call upon our lives.

Each day, I, too, am *Becoming* a Woman of Principle. I am continually transforming my mind, living courageously and rising to my calling.

Becoming is a Transcendent Experience

Through the five practices and principles, we are no longer slaves to fear or unworthiness. Whether you are a rock star CEO, a power-woman in your community, a generous stay-at-home mom or an inspiring woman rebuilding her life, we turn away from the lies we once believed, allowing supernatural truths to renew our minds as we rise into a new level of consciousness and wisdom. We begin to understand we are divinely significant. We humbly accept the challenges we will face as we become honest, *become* our word, *become* servant leaders, *become* champions and *become* wise through God First. As Women of Principle, our lives are the ultimate sermon of love. So, we choose love — every day, everywhere, with everyone, regardless of what they choose.

> *As we become masters in each domain,*
> *we become teachers of the practices.*

This is one of the outcomes of the God First practice. We know that although we will never "perfect" each one, we humbly strive towards excellence based on Romans 12:2, which states, we will be **"transformed by the renewing of our minds."** This life-long commitment gives us the power to impact every single person we meet on the journey towards eternal life.

The Final Distinction

At the heart of each practice, there is one final distinction that is the thread that ties all of this together. This distinction will impact everything in your life, *and I mean everything.*

This final distinction is known as a "declaration." The word declaration means "to make evident, to show."

What we say to ourselves, once or a thousand times, quietly or out loud, will manifest in our lives and the world. Pause and allow me to repeat this statement, "What we say to ourselves, once or a thousand times, quietly or out loud, will manifest in our lives and the world."

Beautiful lady, this is the most powerful moment in the book because "to declare" is the distinction that affirms God's existence. God certainly doesn't have to prove His existence or the truth of the Word. However, the almighty Spirit of Love uses the declaration, "In the beginning, God..." (Genesis 1:1) to introduce himself to mankind. His choice to make a declaration generated everything we know — and don't know.

When we make a declaration and align our declarations with God's promises and His Word, we step into a new possibility. Anything that follows, "I AM," becomes a new experience once you declare it and live into it one word, one behavior, one *transforming* thought at a time. This is true of all declarations. I would bet that your life is the sum total of every thought and every word you have ever spoken. If you experience life with great joy, I bet that your thoughts and words align with how you experience life — most of the time. If you experience life with doubt, anxiety and anger, I bet your thoughts, words and actions reflect the emotions and reactions. Through your God First practice, the supernatural wisdom of the Holy Spirit will be revealed, and your character and *transforming mind* will change. Declarations have creative power, and all declarations generate who we become and how we experience the world. This distinction totally aligns with the five practices. We are co-creators in Christ. Every word we speak generates results.

Allow me to share three examples of how divine declarations work.

Becoming "I AM"

Many in recovery will understand the moment I chose sobriety for a lifetime. I got sober on April 15th. Not on April 14th or any other date. Why? Many would argue reasons, such as a lack of willingness prevent sobriety. I would add another critical distinction: On April 15th, I had *an awareness, and I made a powerful declaration.* The awareness came from the Spirit of God. This new consciousness gave me access to activate my free will and make a powerful declaration. Through the Spirit of Love, I became present to the "distinction called sobriety." As I prayed for healing, the grace of this all-knowing God whispered in my spirit, "sobriety is possible." This one word from God changed my whole life. I used my free will, the power of the Word and my own words to ignite this new life.

Lean in,
DEAR SISTERS.

Despite every bit of evidence that was against me, I humbly declared, "I AM sober. I have the strength to be sober just for today, in Jesus's name."

This declaration of faith, a declaration the size of a mustard seed, gave me the power to create a new experience that wasn't available to me in the days leading up to the 15th.

Listen carefully:

Even when my faith is weak, His promises stand as truth. When I align my small seed of faith and my declaration with His promises, I received supernatural healing. In that one moment, I declared I could live as a sober woman.

I aligned my behaviors and my *transforming mind* to be a sober woman. A declaration takes an iron-clad commitment. Either you are sober, or you are not. Being sober and staying sober is for the individual who lives into their declaration, like a reality, every single day. And, everyone who has ever made their own journey through hell to home knows the *transforming mind* is the key to our freedom. We take action and implement practices to reinforce the declaration. Job or no job, marriage or no marriage, death of a loved one, loss of house or home, big promotion, fame and fortune, we are sober because we say so, like a supernatural declaration.

The same it is with you and any challenge you face in your life. Your declaration will determine your future.

Fat-Ass Tuesdays Open the Door for Transformation

We called our weekly outings "Fat-Ass Tuesdays," because if it wasn't pizza and wings, it was tacos and chips. We had a blast. This tradition went on for years. It is where I fell in love with a young lady named Lisa. *(I want to keep her anonymity, so I won't say much more.)* We met over a slice of pepperoni pizza. Despite her broken heart, she was and is one of the most brilliant and loving women I know.

When she and I began working together, she could hardly speak. She had a very difficult time completing a few sentences. The abuse she endured during her childhood and as a young woman left her riddled with anxiety and 100 forms of fear. Her addictions included all kinds of alcohol and drugs, and her mindset was addicted to confusion and negativity. I had never met anyone who had suffered so many life-altering challenges — other than me — and lived to tell about them. At first, I was overwhelmed with concern for her well-being, and I wasn't sure I had the wisdom she needed to be her mentor. But our God, mighty in nature, had another plan. She and I began the work of recovery and the practice of faith, the size of a mustard seed. One conversation at a time, we uncovered the broken pieces of her past and aligned her warrior's heart with the bold promises of God. The women in the program and the church surrounded her with love and every act of kindness until she loved herself. She began to declare her own possibilities. Eventually, she believed her declarations. She not only declared, "I AM sober," but many other declarations that have since come true. Declarations like, "I AM a college student," "I AM a social worker," "I AM reunited with my family," "I AM worthy of love," and many others, which are now a reality in her life.

Lisa aligned her life with the practices of honesty, running with champions and God First. She aligned her declarations with the principles of God. Today, her life is beyond her wildest dreams. Lisa "is" an "I AM" *Becoming* Woman of Principle — a living testimony of the *transforming mind*. She is victorious and is dedicated to bringing the next woman into the arms of God. She aligned her faith — the size of a mustard seed — and her bold declarations with the truths of God. I am honored that I was a central part of her life for more than five years. I love you, Lisa, and I still love pepperoni pizza.

Courage for Christ

My dear friend Holli is another *Becoming* Woman of Principle. I am proud to serve as her spiritual mentor, as well. When Holli came into my life, she had recently lost her fiancé to a motorcycle accident. To say she was heartbroken would be an understatement. It was a crushing, life-altering event. She and I have spent many evenings together, as she processed the "why" behind such a devastating loss in her life. We would cry, pray and trust that she would receive a peace that surpasses all understanding. The other women in her tribe would hold Holli in their arms until the wave of fear passed. Despite her grief and anger, Holli persevered one day at a time. She is one of the bravest women I have ever known. Holli began attending Christ Fellowship Church with us every Saturday evening. It was in the presence of the Spirit of Love that we witnessed Holli *Become* a Woman of Principle. As she practiced God First through prayer and praise and worship, she began to experience joy. She practiced being her word and practiced a new level of honesty with everyone. Her *transforming mind* shifted towards servant leadership, and the principle of generosity became her guide. It was through this unbearable incident that the God of her understanding inspired her to pursue a ministry degree. Holli began declaring, "I AM a woman with a missionary's heart," and "I AM my word." She declared it and began acting in alignment with her declarations. She started a group called Courage for Christ. Although it cannot replace Craig, the mission to serve fills her soul, and she is a contribution to the community. Holli is an "I AM" Woman of Principle. Holli, you reflect God's grace, and you are one of the dearest women I have ever known. I love you.

And, so it is with you, Women of Principle. No matter what you face, you can be an "I AM" Woman of Principle.

The choice is yours.

When conflict arises, practice choosing your "I AM" declaration.

We have chosen the declarations:

I am beautifully transparent

I am impeccable

I am generous

I am honest

I am my word

I am wise

You can declare others as well.

I made another personal declaration a long time ago:

> **"I AM** *a powerful, authentic, trusting,*
> *spiritual Woman of Principle."*

This is who I am and how I am committed to showing up. I may not always do this perfectly, but this is my commitment. When I fail to show up in this way, I make amends and get in alignment with my promise to be a stand for love. It has become that easy. What we practice, we become.

What is your declaration, beautiful lady?
Who are you committed to being in the world?

THE  Journey HOME

Dearest Women of Principle,

In closing, I am deeply honored you have trusted me by taking the journey through hell to home — to transforming, living and rising — together.

The time has come for you to rise and live courageously. Will you say, "Yes!" to the call upon your life?

Are you ready to shed the behaviors, thoughts and language that make it impossible for your transforming mind to accomplish your dreams? The world is waiting for women, just like you. There is a child seeking words of encouragement, a waitress longing to know she is loved, a co-worker who has never known grace, or perhaps a stranger in line at the grocery store who feels completely alone. You are the light of God — every day, everywhere, with everyone. You are the everyday Woman of Principle.

When we make the commitment to practice this new way of being and decide —every day, everywhere with everyone — we become an entirely new set of thoughts, words and actions. We become a new creation in Christ.

My hope for every beautiful lady reading this book is that you will accept the invitation to know God, His son, Jesus, and the love of the Holy Spirit. I pray you will allow your transforming mind to understand the promises of God. And, more than anything else, I pray you know, beyond a shadow of a doubt, that you are loved, wonderfully and beautifully made, and your life matters. God can take us from failures — big and small — to success and to divine significance. You are worthy, dear sisters.

I pray that through this book, Becoming Woman of Principle: Transforming Your Mind, Living Courageously and Rising to Your Call, we will create a movement where 1 million women will come to know God intimately, master the practices, accept the call upon their lives and RISE — as a stand for love, every day, everywhere, for everyone.

This call is for all women to experience the fulfillment that only comes through being aligned with your divine significance. On behalf of the Spirit of the Lord, I ask, "Will you be a champion in the world?"

Go in peace and practice becoming who God has called you to be.

Remember, "We all, with unveiled face, beholding as the mirror of the Lord, are being transformed into the same image, from glory to glory, just as by the spirit of the Lord."

Whoever you are, wherever you are, it is time to rise to your call. May you always be blessed on your journey, and may that journey always bring you HOME. Selah.

In grace and glory,

M.K.

MEET
MARY KATHERINE MORALES (M.K.)

I am an author, trainer, accomplished professional and visionary leader. For the past 15 years, I've been inspiring women - just like you - to embrace their divine purpose and live their dreams!

Today, I am an authentic, fun-loving, spiritual leader who is transforming, living and rising as a Woman of Principle - every day!

However, my life wasn't always so inspiring!

When I was 14 and the Spirit of God literally gave me the direction that I would write a book, I had absolutely no idea it would be a book based on my failures.

I heard the call a second time in my thirties while suffering as an addict. I was literally shouting to God for help and the Holy Spirit almost audibly stated, "You will recover, and you will write a book about your journey through hell to home."

Yeah, right was my response.

I swore I would never tell anyone about the degree to which I failed - repeatedly.

Not only did God command me to share my story of victory in a small room with those who can relate to my trials, but to the world. My purpose is to provide the kind of power that lies in storytelling and transparency so that shame steps into the light of God and unworthiness bows to a bold new identity through the Spirit of Love.

Why? Because there is only one you, and only you can bring your unique purpose to the world.

JOIN US ON THE JOURNEY AND
DISCOVER YOUR
divine significance

www.womanofprinciple.com

Want to learn more?

Email: **becomingwop@gmail.com**

Chat with Mary Katherine:

561-951-3450

Find us on social media:

@ **Women of Principle**